Advance Praise for *Controlled*

"With hauntingly vivid detail, Neesha Arter's *Controlled* brings the trauma of surviving sexual assault to life. In the midst of profound pain, she finds indefatigable courage—a force so palpable it stays with you long after the final page. Fearless, intimate and strikingly honest, it's a gripping tale not simply of survival, but the refusal to be silenced. Her first memoir is rife with suffering and bursting at the seams with hope. I felt it in my bones—and still do."

— Abby Haglage (*The Daily Beast*)

"Neesha Arter's honest, no holds barred account of stolen innocence is an important entry into understanding the sexual violence so many girls and women experience. Arter not only illustrates the devastating effects of her assault, the familial betrayal she faced, and her own self-harm, but also chronicles how she conquered these tremendous adversities. *Controlled* depicts the power of a young woman who chose to own her story."

— Lane Florsheim (*Marie Claire*)

"Neesha Arter puts a name, a face and a riveting, rocking, shame-free and utterly gifted writing voice to an all-too-common female coming-of-age experience, sexual assault. Required reading for parents and educators and especially for teen boys and men who care about women and girls."

— Nina Burleigh (Bestselling Author of *The Fatal Gift of Beauty: The Trials of Amanda Knox*)

"*Controlled* reveals the true courage needed to face terrible experiences, by so many young women around the world. Neesha's brave spirit should be a beacon of hope for others and her compelling account, while harrowing in places, will enlist   ."

— Sarah Kennedy (*New York Observer*)

D1490519

"I haven't come across so much bravery, honesty and flat-out gutsy writing in a long time. Neesha Arter tackles a difficult subject with grace and simply gorgeous writing. Her beautiful prose soothes the hard edges of the story she tells. She has the ability to bring the reader very close and hold us there for the entire length of the book. You won't be able to put this one down. A stunning debut."
—Margot Berwin (Bestselling Author of *Hothouse Flower and the Nine Plants of Desire*)

"Neesha's powerful words send an impactful message that stay with you long after reading. She reminds us to always listen to our instinct, do not rationalize."
—Laurice Rahme (United Nations Women for Peace Association Peace Award recipient / Founder of Bond No. 9 New York)

"While much media about sexual assault focuses on the college arena, Arter's courageous *Controlled* reminds us that these issues start much earlier. A crucially important read."
—Annie E. Clark (Co-Founder, End Rape on Campus)

"Neesha Arter provides a relatable voice for countless victims of sexual assault and the trauma that tends to occur as a result. While *Controlled* is filled with graphic descriptions and painful discoveries, it's a gripping story that will serve as a lesson to those who have been Arter's shoes and those who have never encountered this hardship."
—Dena Silver (*New York Observer*)

"With great bravery and wonderful prose Neesha Arter recalls her own ordeal. This memoir of her journey will help bring to light issues that affect so many women around the world, and inspire other survivors of sexual assault to break their silence."
—Jennifer Wright (Author of *It Ended Badly*)

"Neesha Arter's courage to tell her story of sexual assault is incredibly urgent given the prevalence of this issue. Her bravery to speak forth and share her story opens the doors for many others that are in similar shoes. Arter gives hope to so many people in this world and she is a young voice we desperately need."

—Jessica White (Model)

"Arter exposes the sexist mindset that boys will be boys and girls will be sluts. Her post-sexual assault downward spiral is chilling. This book is a must-read for anyone who wants to understand the terrors of sexual assault and the slut-shaming that so often follows."

—Leora Tanenbaum (Author of *I Am Not a Slut: Slut-Shaming in the Age of the Internet*)

"Neesha Arter writes a brave memoir that needs to be read. *Controlled* is an honest and unflinching portrayal of a young girl's trauma written with a mature, deft hand. This is a brilliant debut and I will be awaiting more from this talented author."

—Lee Matthew Goldberg (Author of *Slow Down* and the upcoming *The Mentor*)

"Neesha's writing is gripping and powerful. The intensity of the story pulls you in from page one and squeezes your heart and angers your mind. Arter's journey is one of suffering, triumph and inspiration, and its message echoes loud and clear. After reading *Controlled*, you quite literally, will find yourself speechless."

—Sunny Tripathy (Mr. India Global / Screenwriter/ Producer at 20th Century Fox)

"Neesha Arter's *Controlled* is a darkly sparkling vision. A soulful journey about seeking light and self-acceptance while honoring the pain that makes us stronger. Arter is a vivid, triumphant voice that demands to be heard."

—Royal Young (Author of *Fame Shark*)

"*Controlled* will grab ahold of anyone who has recovered from trauma. Neesha Arter, part of the *Brave Miss World* team, helped share our film's message of the importance of speaking out about sexual assault and now courageously faces her own darkest memory to tell a powerful story of emerging into the light."

—Cecilia Peck (Emmy nominated director of *Brave Miss World*)

"As a male survivor of sexual assault, I firmly believe it is important we speak out. Neesha Arter does a phenomenal job of providing a compelling tale of human endurance and redemption. Through her powerful narrative, Neesha breaks the silence on sexual violence while providing hope for a future where no one has to endure this type of pain."

—Tim Mousseau (Writer, Speaker, Storyteller)

"*Controlled* is sure to inspire, empower and enlighten readers of all ages and backgrounds. Neesha Arter shows her bravery, poise and unbreakable spirit through her first memoir, recounting experiences that no one should have to endure. It is clear that Neesha's work of instilling hope and courage in others has just begun and *Controlled* will leave everyone waiting for her next story."

—David Stark (Author of *The Art Of The Party*)

"*Controlled* is the most powerful memoir I have ever read. Neesha courageously invites us to journey with her through the horrors of the night she was raped and her self-destructive attempts to cope with the resultant trauma. Her exceptional gift for writing makes her account intensely vivid and haunting, yet ultimately, hopeful. Any man who wants to be an ally to women and girls who have been raped or assaulted needs to read Neesha's story."

—Eugene Hung (Man Up Campaign)

Controlled

THE WORST
NIGHT
OF MY LIFE
AND ITS
AFTERMATH

NEESHA ARTER

 Heliotrope Books

New York

Heliotrope Books LLC
heliotropebooks@gmail.com

Cover photograph by Celeste Sloman

Designed and typeset by Naomi Rosenblatt with AJJ Design

For the past ten years we have learned the hard way.
Mom and Dad, do not ever think you did less than
  an unbelievable job.
We made it.
And here it is.

Author's Note

In order to provide anonymity, the names and identifying details of some characters in this book have been changed.

"We all survive more than we think we can."
—Joan Didion

FOREWORD

This is a story you need to hear.

It happened in a country where a woman's chances of being raped are one in five—the United States of America.

It happened to a girl of fourteen. And the offenders were people she knew.

To a mother of daughters, Neesha Arter's account is a nightmare. Her words are not easy to read. They might make you cry, or cry out. But ten years later, Neesha has already made something positive of having endured this horrific crime. Her story is an example of the true recovery that comes with strength and perseverance. It speaks to who she is and offers hope to others.

When I met Neesha, she was twenty-two years old and covering a FREEDOM FOR ALL event for the *New York Observer*. I was drawn to her passion for helping victims of rape. FREEDOM FOR ALL is the nonprofit I founded to combat human trafficking and forced labor. I see in Neesha a fellow warrior for the dignity of lives reclaimed.

Neesha's book holds value for a great variety of readers: victims—female and male—seeking support and perspective, parents and teachers of teenagers, those who struggle with eating disorders, those seeking to enforce protective laws, and young men learning to behave respectfully with women.

Victims of rape are frequently silenced or, even worse, blamed. Neesha emphasizes the the importance of listening to those who've been violated and urging them to share their truths openly. She has written a story we all need to hear and talk about until it ceases to happen ever again.

Katie Ford
Founder, FREEDOM FOR ALL
Former CEO, Ford Models

PRELUDE ∘ december, 2006

There's a soft sound in here, the sort of sound that no one can hear but you—the sort of sound you feel. It's the hum you make up in your head when the boy you like brushes your hair out of your face with his fingers and kisses you. I hear something ever so faint, but it might just be the immense silence of my room. My shoulder quivers as if someone tapped me, but no one's here. I am alone with this memory.

On my fourteenth New Year's Eve, the only desire I knew was longing for the boy I liked to touch my hand as he walked by. I was petite and pretty then—or at least I thought I was—with long, straight, black hair and dark brown eyes against my tanned Indian skin. But on that New Year's Eve, a chilly night in Houston, I secretly wished for even more smoldering looks. I could never have imagined that by the next morning my dreams would be shattered, my mind poisoned, and my body raped.

Before that night, a year ago now, I never once pictured myself as the victim. Yet, as I look at my familiar bedroom walls and feel the weight of pink cotton sheets on my motionless body, I'm transported back to Houston. The sheets feel scratchy against my skin, but I don't move to adjust them. It hurts too much to look at my own body. Inadvertently, I spot my kneecaps poking through the thin material and the sight makes me tremble. The white curtains that have shut out the world remain closed, leaving me alone in my claustrophobic room.

A ray of light peers through the curtains, but still this room feels like a trap. I want to escape from this room. I want to escape from that night. I can't.

That New Year's Eve, the threshold of 2006, brings with it the shaking apprehension I felt all last year, when I was fourteen. That night I remember shuddering, but most of all I remember the paralysis, the terror of being violated. As I toss and turn in these pink sheets, those feelings plague me once again.

My body tingles like it would on a first date, except there's no excitement or anticipation. I rub my stinging eyes, but I cannot rub away the image of the boys' faces. As I lie here, I don't feel like myself. Something's wrong. My heartbeat won't slow down. Bubbles and bubbles fill my stomach; like adding baking soda to vinegar, they just keep overflowing, but I am here alone.

1 ∘ december 31, 2005

A group of us girls sat on one of the couches in the living room eating chips: my cousin Anita's friends from school—Lisa and Kate—and me. Anita, my closest cousin, the sister I never had, stood across the room with her older brother, Rob.

"Hey, what movie do you guys want to watch?"

Such an inconsequential question, but it's the first clear thing I remember about that night. My cousin Rob looked over at Mark and Will as he asked it. Rob, two years older and cooler, was always off with his best friend, Mark. I had grown close to Mark over the years, and like Rob, he treated me like a little sister. He always gave me the best hugs, asked me about volleyball, and wanted to know if I had a new favorite movie. I didn't; it was still *Miss Congeniality*. I loved this sweet charm he had about him. I'm sure every girl dreamed about being with him, but I had never thought of Mark in that way. As boy-crazy as I was, I never felt the urge to kiss him or anything like that, but I will admit he wasn't bad to look at with his dark skin and those piercing golden-brown eyes. Mark was tall, like all the boys, but I knew him all my life and always thought of him as a little kid. Rob and Mark were practically brothers. They bought the newest video games every time a new one came out and would play it for hours while Anita and I would be outside passing a volleyball back and forth. We shared our passion for the sport and both played the same position: setter.

I glanced at the black clock. It read 11:00 p.m.—one hour until the New Year!

"I don't know," Will said. "Anything."

"Anita, come over here," I yelled across the room. "I want to talk to you."

I waited until she walked over, her black hair bouncing behind her in a tight ponytail. She settled down on the couch between Kate and me.

"Do you think Will's cute?" I whispered, blushing. I did—I thought he was the most beautiful boy I had ever seen. With dark brown eyes and the longest eyelashes that flicked in my direction, he didn't look like any of the boys I knew from my school. He had a sharp jawline like the actors do in the movies, and his hair fell perfectly, though it was slightly short—not a buzz cut but not quite long enough to run your fingers through it. Will was older, maybe even one year older than Rob, and almost six feet tall. He wore dark jeans and a fitted button-down black shirt. "I can't stop staring at him."

Anita's eyes lit up, and a smile spread across her face. "Neesha! Yes. You guys would be perfect together. He's older, cooler. More mature."

"He's like seventeen!"

"Exactly."

"I don't know if he even likes me."

"He totally does. Rob was telling me that he thinks you're cute."

I felt my blush return and excitement dancing through my whole being. "No way!"

"Yes!"

I glowed. "I so hope you're right."

The movie *Fight Club* started playing in the background as everyone sipped champagne out of plastic red cups. The giant living room had four different couches in it and the biggest flat-screen television I'd ever seen. Leather chairs and glass coffee tables made me feel so adult, and champagne bubbles tickled my tongue when I took a few sips. The stereo system played music in all ten rooms of my aunt and uncle's house, including the kitchen. It was like being in a hotel, right down to the water slide in the backyard pool and the massive sauna.

With fifteen minutes to go, we turned off the movie in favor of the New Year's Eve countdown. We all topped off our champagne and laughed away the last strokes of the year. I stood between Anita and Rob, each with an arm wrapped around me. As the clock struck midnight, we jumped up and down in tipsy glee.

"Happy New Year!" we shouted in unison, and I hugged both my cousins.

I glanced over Rob's shoulder across the room to find Will staring at me, his eyes twinkling. "Happy New Year," he mouthed as he winked at me. My heart somersaulted in my chest in the most childish way, and I knew he was my new crush.

We settled down onto the couches and put the movie back on. An hour or so went by before I heard a creak and saw the front door open. Rob and Anita's parents—my aunt and uncle—walked into the living room, all smiles as they passed through on the way to their bedroom. We used to play the most intensive games of hide and seek when we were younger because there were so many clever hiding spots in this house. I would usually hide in my aunt's closet in the very back corner behind all her saris and Indian scarves, but the options were endless with two floors of rooms.

"Happy New Year!" my uncle yelled.

"Happy New Year!" we shouted back.

My aunt paused in the hallway. "You guys really should go to bed soon. I'm sure everyone's had a long night."

"Okay, Mom," Rob said, mild irritation in his tone.

"I mean it, kids," my aunt insisted.

Rob let out a big sigh but clicked off the television by remote. "Fine, we heard you."

She smiled at her son, and then she gave the rest of us a wave. "Good night everybody!"

Rob sat up and stretched, then he fell back onto the couch. "You guys just want to sleep in here?" he asked Mark and Will.

They did.

Anita and I walked to her room with Lisa and Kate. Their giggles were subdued as everyone changed into their pajamas and climbed into Anita's bed. After a while, Lisa and Anita slept in her bed, while Kate and I both had sleeping bags on the floor. As kids, Anita, Rob and I used to have sleepovers in her room as if we were camping, tucked into our favorite sleeping bags; mine was a perfect shade of blueberry blue, and here I was snuggled up in it again. Moving back and forth, I remembered those days that felt like everything was simple. At that moment it still did. I turned to look at the bed and saw the girls now resting, their murmurs ceased and their breathing slow and even. I shifted my legs beneath my sleeping bag and stared at the clock. It was 2:04 a.m., but I wasn't the slightest bit sleepy—and I couldn't get Will out of my head. His eyes glimmered in the darkness of my mind, his smile brightened my face, and his wink sent shivers up and down my spine.

Rustling around for a couple minutes longer, I realized I couldn't bear the curiosity of what he was doing anymore. I slid out of my sleeping bag and tiptoed from Anita's room back to the living room.

"Not the best New Year's," Mark complained as I crept down the hallway.

The floor creaked beneath my feet. Mark and Will jerked their heads toward me. Blushing, I came out from behind the wall.

"Oh, hey, Neesha." Will smiled. "What are you doing up?"

"I can't sleep." I returned the older boy's smile. "What about you guys?"

Will muttered something, but I couldn't catch his words. My confidence started to falter. I dropped my eyes to his shadow and shifted my weight from foot to foot. I was wearing my favorite red volleyball shirt from the summer camp I went to the year before, with black-and-white striped pajama pants. Beneath that favorite shirt was a black bra from Victoria's Secret and matching pink lace underwear.

"Did you have a good night, Neesha?" Mark asked me.

He appeared the same as always, with a look of care, almost brotherly, but when I lifted my gaze I saw a grin I had never seen before. I didn't like that grin; it made the hair on the back of my neck stand straight up.

"Yeah," I said uneasily. "It was really good."

"Nice…" Mark said, with sort of a snotty tone.

Will came over to me and grabbed my hand. "Come with me, Neesha—I want to show you something."

What could I do but follow?

As he led me out of the room, I wondered what he could possibly want to show me in the rarely-used exercise room. But I didn't say anything, didn't listen to that little voice of warning inside my head. I could only focus on the feel of his fingers wrapped so tightly around my hand. Moonlight peeked through the blinds as we stepped into the chilly room. It was dark and smelled like new exercise equipment, almost like the scent of a new car, but more rubbery. A yoga mat leaned against the wall, still in its plastic wrapping. I could barely make out the color since there was such little light, but I thought it might be red. Double-glass windows to the left, a white door to the right, another door behind me, the boys in front of me—both of them now, though I hadn't noticed Mark following us. I tried not to dwell on how the plain white walls enclosed me like a cage. Instead I looked at a brand-new treadmill pushed up against one wall, already shrouded in a thin layer of dust. The room felt colder than the rest of the house, probably because the door was always closed.

"Doesn't anyone in this family work out?" I joked uncomfortably.

Will let go of my hand and took a step back toward the door. He turned its lock clockwise. The click it made somehow sounded definite or final. I knew from all my visits to my cousins' house that the other door behind us led only to a bathroom—no escape there. My stomach cramped as I realized I was trapped.

"Please," I whispered to myself, "get me out of here."

Will sat down on an exercise bench and patted the seat next to him, while Mark leaned back against the wall. My knees were wobbly as I stepped toward Will, but I told myself I was just overreacting. These boys were my friends, and this was a safe place, the home of my cousins, of my aunt and uncle.

But just as I sat down, Will began to unbutton his dark jeans.

My heart dropped and my stomach turned. "I think I should go," I whispered, looking away from his crotch.

"What? Why?" His free hand took my chin and turned my face toward his. In the moonlight his eyes glittered. "Don't you like me, Neesha?"

No, I thought, not at all—not anymore. "I just—I really need to go."

My body felt so heavy, my muscles so weak. I used every bit of strength I had to pull myself to my feet, but Will grabbed the back of my neck. My knees buckled, and I fell helplessly onto the bench.

"Don't be like that," Will cooed next to me. His fingernails dug into the skin on my neck. "Please, just give me head."

I swallowed the nothing that was in my dry mouth. From out of my throat came my scratchy voice: "I've never done that. I really need—"

"It's really not that difficult," he interrupted. His nails dug deeper into my skin. "Just try it."

I closed my lips and bit them as hard as I could. Staring into those brown eyes that I thought were so beautiful just a few moments ago, I now only wanted to be somewhere away from Will—somewhere far, far away from this room. Anywhere but here. But I was too terrified to move. My fear held me in place as if I had a gun pointed at me; my trembling body was turned to leave. My heart raced out of my chest and breathing was out of the question.

A lightweight, red cotton blanket had been lying on the floor beside the workout bench, which I noticed when we walked into the room. Will reached down to grab it, and then he threw it over my back. I couldn't figure out why, but the more I started to panic the more I began shaking. In some small part of me that was still calm, I thought I had a fever; my blood was boiling, my skin sweating, and all this seemed like a fever-induced hallucination. I shook my body free of the blanket and turned to look for Mark, but Will took my face in one hand and with the other pulled my long hair. Salty tears rushed to my eyes as he forced my face down to his crotch. I bit my lips together harder, but suddenly my mouth was full. He pushed his penis down into my throat while pulling hard on my hair, but when I tried to pull my hair back my arms felt numb. Two tears began to stream down my face.

And then two hundred tears.

I choked and gagged as Will forced himself into my mouth over and over. I tried to turn my head again to look for Mark, but Will held me firmly in place with his hand tangled in my black hair.

I felt someone pulling off my pajama pants. While Will continued to stick his penis in my mouth, Mark shoved his fingers inside my vagina.

Frozen solid yet so hot beneath the blanket, I didn't move. I couldn't move. My body felt paralyzed in a way I had never felt before.

So far removed from that moment as I now lie here in this uncomfortable bed, I haven't forgiven myself for that—for not fighting, for not struggling. I don't know if I ever will.

Like a whirlwind, I tried to move my body and get up to leave, but fear filled my eyes as I tried to lift myself up. I remember my ninety-pound body shaking as if it were freezing. The only movement I could manage was to turn around and look at Mark right in the face while Will adjusted his own body. Each time I did that, he would stop fingering me and start to walk away. But as soon as Will twisted my head back around, Mark's fingers would attack me again.

Yet the worst of the shaking was in my mind. I remember saying that I needed to go or trying to say it as Will shoved his penis down my throat. "I am going," I remember trying to say, as though my conviction would make it happen. I remember trying to get up and leave, but I couldn't move. My legs had never felt heavier. My boiling heart felt like it was going to explode as it radiated the only heat I could feel. Worst of all, I remember my body shutting off, my mind shutting off. All of me shut off.

I hurt. I will never forget the scraping feeling of Mark fingering me; every time his nails dug into me, fresh terror rushed through my whole body. My eyes, alive with helpless fear, surely would have made any normal person stop. Didn't he see my eyes? I had never felt this type of pain before. Every violated part of my body hurt. My eyes watered, and my nose felt like it had been punched out in a boxing ring. I tried to scream as loud as I possibly could around Will's assault, but no one heard me. No sound would come out of my mouth except a cough.

I turned my eyes to the window to look out at the dark night, but even then I could feel how hopeless my stare was. I wanted nothing more than to jump out the window to freedom and escape from this hell.

Someone, please save me.

I had only my shirt on. Two in the morning, maybe three, and I wished so badly I had just gone to sleep with the other girls. The disturbing motions and movements of the three of us carried on for what seemed like hours.

Please take me away from here.

Mark, my friend for years, someone I trusted, completely disregarded my pleading stare. I could not look at him again. Didn't he know he was hurting me? Didn't he know I would hurt for years?

"Let me put it in," Will groaned above me. "Put it in, Neesha. Just a few seconds. It won't hurt."

Inside my spinning head, I screamed "NO!" over and over again—as if I had a choice at this point. My heart must have been racing, but I couldn't even feel it beating. Was this how I was going to lose my virginity?

Please stop.

My body felt limp, and I thought at any moment I could throw up. Letting out a quick cough, my naked knees scratched the carpet, and I was sure some of the pizza I ate earlier would be on the floor soon. I could taste bitter saliva forming in my mouth as my jaw stung.

I had never felt so wronged. I had never even had a first real kiss or a real boyfriend. This wasn't supposed to be how it happened. I knew that much.

Above me, Will kept on with that question, over and over: "Can I just be in you for a few seconds? Nothing will happen. Please."

"No," I gagged. "Puh, please no—just stop."

"No, it's fine, just let me finish like this. Just let me finish. Come on!"

Did he not get it? Did he really think he was giving me a choice? With his hand intertwined in my long black hair, I could feel strands of it coming loose in his grip. I lifted my shaking hands to the back of my head and placed them over his hand, summoning the strength to at least try to pull his hands away to loosen his grip.

A crack of light from the bathroom caught my eye, and I saw Mark's shadow move across the open door. I had not even realized he stopped assaulting me, so mind-numbing was my terror. Wasn't he going to help me? Wasn't he going to make this stop now?

Suddenly I heard a click from the other door—the click of a lock moving. The door opened to reveal the silhouetted figure of my aunt as light flooded over me. Will's hands let my head go as I quickly turned to squint through my tears, the first time in minutes my face hadn't been pressed forcibly to Will's crotch, but I could not see her face.

"Neesha! What are you doing?"

2 ∘ *a blessing and a curse*
sunday, january 1, 2006

My half-naked body, still more or less covered by the red blanket, went numb, but I could not have been more relieved when I saw my aunt at that moment, as shameful as it was. The worst nightmare I could have ever imagined was finally over.

She saved me.

But even as Will leapt backward from me, at last freeing my mouth, I knew it wasn't over. I knew pain like that would not just disappear. The pain was deeper than simply the acts that took place. The torment became a part of me the moment it ended.

I breathed a sigh of relief, so happy that I wouldn't have to be in the same room as these disgusting creatures any longer. But then, fear seized me again. What would my aunt do? What would she think of me?

"Oh my gosh," I whispered to myself, again and again. I fumbled for my pajama pants and slipped them on my broken body as fast as I could. Will buttoned up his jeans as my aunt looked away and took a step toward the door. As she turned around, I put my messy long, black hair up in a bun with the pink hair tie on my wrist and then placed my head in my hands. Standing up, I noticed my body shook more than it did in the past hour, but I pushed by everyone and headed toward

Anita's room in a hurry.

Walking down the hall, I opened the door to find the girls asleep. Rummaging through my things, I found my phone and crept back into the hallway to call the only friend I thought would be awake at that hour: Jane, one of my best friends.

"Hey, it's me. I really need you to call me as soon as you can. I have to tell you something. It's really not good, but I have to tell you. I can't believe this just happened. Please call me back. Thanks," I said in a traumatized tone on her voicemail.

I thought about texting my other two best friends—Emma and Brad—but I couldn't even type out the words to explain what happened. Brad had always been the boy in my life that I trusted, but it felt too awkward to tell him something like this. Emma had been my closest best friend for years, and she knew everything about me, but for some reason I feared her reaction. Maybe it was because she kept everything to herself, and I had always been the overly sensitive girl that took everything to heart. What would she say? I didn't know if I was strong enough to tell her.

Unaware of how to feel when I took my phone back to Anita's room, I tried to pull myself together before I went downstairs to face Will and my aunt. "It's okay," I told myself repeatedly. "Just explain what happened. Will has to come clean. You didn't do anything wrong, anyway."

I found Will and my aunt seated at the kitchen table. Neither greeted me as I took a seat several chairs away from the boy I had been so smitten with only a few hours ago.

Finally my aunt broke the silence. "Would you like to tell me what happened, Neesha?"

Far too ashamed to say anything, I stared at the table. Unable to look anyone in the eyes, I just looked down.

"She started it," Will said in the wake of my silence. "She came on to me the whole night. I had no control over any part of this situation."

Was he serious?

My heart raced as fast as it would on the Tower of Terror at

Disneyland. I could not believe he was putting the blame on me. The possibility of him lying had never even crossed my mind. How could I be so stupid? Of course he could lie, but my naïveté had taken over.

"You're lying!" I sputtered. How could he be so heartless? He had the straightest face I'd ever seen on a liar, and in hindsight I had an urge to pat him on the back for it. I never could have lied like that.

"Okay, Neesha," my aunt said as Will stared straight into my eyes. She gave me a look of disapproval with her dark brown eyes that I had never seen before. Growing up, I always admired her and thought her beauty made her perfect. She had light brown skin and gorgeous dark brown hair that always looked flawless. She appeared put-together in a way I hoped to be when I was older. Never did I think I would see an ugly side of her.

She was the "cool" aunt, the one who let me eat too many cookies and buy impractical shoes that my mom would never allow. She had always been more traditional than my mom, more religious, and was always watching one of her favorite Indian movies that I could never really understand. However, what I loved about her the most was that I could talk to her about anything. "Why don't you tell me what happened," she said.

I took a deep breath and tried to pick up my pieces.

The pieces of me that were left in the exercise room that night.

The pieces of me now on the kitchen table and in my chair.

But most of all, the pieces of me that I lost when I looked into the eyes of Will and Mark while they invaded my body.

They'd taken those pieces, and I knew I wasn't getting them back.

Trying to tell myself that my life would fit together again, my mind filled with dread over whether or not I would get in trouble. But my aunt would believe me over Will, I was sure. After all, family was supposed to stick together, right?

I was so angry with the two boys and with myself as I tried to tell my aunt what happened, so furious at the whole situation. "Look, I didn't do—"

"What? This was completely your doing," Will said.

"I just went to talk to them and I—"

"You came in there because you liked me. We all knew that the whole night."

"That doesn't even matter…" I tried to continue.

Will then stood up and left the table.

"Neesha, you need to just stop making excuses," scolded my aunt.

"No! Stop, that's not true—this was his fault!" Seconds passed in silence once I tried to catch my breath through my tears. I rubbed my face with my hands, waiting for my aunt to offer some words of comfort.

"How could you disrespect us like this, in our own home?" she demanded. "How could you do this to me and your uncle?"

My heart plummeted. "I didn't do—"

Her eyes were cold. "You are completely in the wrong! Why weren't you in bed like you were supposed to be? If you had gone to sleep like we told you, none of this would have happened!"

"But I—"

"Go to bed," she snapped. "It's the middle of the night, and I can't even look at you right now. Just go upstairs and go to sleep."

She couldn't seriously believe him. "Oh my god," I said to myself in shock.

I stumbled up the stairs like a beaten dog. I crawled into the sleeping bag as quietly as possible. How could this night have gotten so much worse?

A few hours later, around nine in the morning, I woke up and touched my cheeks, wet with bitter tears. I couldn't look in the mirror at my swollen face, but more than anything, I couldn't look at my body. When I went to the bathroom to pee, it burned. I looked in the toilet to see a mix of blood and urine. Flushing quickly, I felt disgusting, ashamed, and dirty. I trembled and shook in my trauma. I began to rationalize my feelings and convinced myself that I just had chills.

I had a bull's eye across my face.

I tried to quit caring.

I sat on a couch downstairs that morning and said nothing and looked at no one. I had nothing to say to any of them. My aunt had not believed me, so why would my cousins? Or anyone else? My aunt yelled into the living room, "Neesha, you need to go talk to your uncle! He's in his room."

I took a deep breath and nodded. Walking over to my aunt and uncle's bedroom, I clenched my hands. I had no desire to hear what he had to say, and I knew he wouldn't believe me anyway. Taking short little steps over to his room, I swallowed the saliva in my mouth. I felt more nervous than I had ever felt before in this house.

Growing up, I used to confide in my uncle, but this walk felt like my feet were sinking into thick mud. Like a walk of shame, since I knew he was not about to side with me over the boys. With more effort, I mustered up all the strength in my body to lift my feet. It was almost like a desperate attempt to free myself, but I could not get away from this conversation.

As a kid I was carefree and easygoing, but occasionally I would get a nervous feeling in my chest, a quick, heavy pounding. Whether it was before a test or before getting a shot at the doctor, I couldn't shake the fear. But no matter how terrified I used to be, I never cried. I would be trembling, but the tears would never come. Even in the tiny window of my weakness, I never let more than two or three glistening tears down my cheeks.

When I finally finished taking about fifteen steps down the hall, I turned into their room to see a California King bed made up with dark red beaded sheets. My aunt always decorated everything in lavish Indian prints and fabrics. Glancing around the room, I noticed my uncle in the bathroom shaving his black facial hair with an electronic razor. He then wiped his face with a fancy white-and-gold towel.

My mind drifted back to Thanksgiving the month before. I remembered putting on my aunt's most extravagant saris and fancy designer high heels with Anita. As we made a mess of her oversized closet, we put on our own little fashion show while blasting the radio. Pretending we were on the most coveted catwalk as a new Kelly Clarkson track blasted, we ended up tripping over the thousand-dollar stilettoes, but we had never laughed so hard together. Tangling up the vibrant yellow and pink scarves, my visits represented the splendor of carelessness and innocence. To me, they were endless fun and gave me the ability to act my age, but the best part was being with the people I loved the most: my family. I remembered the conversation with my family in Houston about my coming on this trip. Rob had never been so excited about anything as he asked my uncle, "Hey dad, wouldn't it be great if Neesha came for New Year's Eve this year?"

"Yes! She has to come!" Anita agreed.

"You and Mom could still go to that party with all your friends, and we'll do our own thing here. Neesha has to be here—we'd have so much fun!" Rob said.

"We'd love that," my uncle answered. "Neesha, how would you like that, sweetie?"

"I'd love it, too!" I turned to my mom, excitement bubbling through me. "Mom, please, please can I come for New Year's?"

"I'll have to think about it. I don't know if it's the best idea. You've never flown by yourself, honey," she told me.

"Oh, she's fine. We'll take care of her. She's our second daughter, you know that, sis. We would never let anything happen to her," my uncle said.

"I know. I know you guys would take great care of her, but I just get nervous," my mom said.

"But Mom, I will be fine." I remember saying with such assertion that I was grown up.

"Neesha, you're still so young. Maybe you should just wait till next year."

"Please, Mom! It will be fine."

I never thought I should have listened to her.

But as I sat down on my uncle's bed, now over a month later, the flashback faded and reality hit. My uncle walked over and did not give off the loving vibe he usually did. He now stood in front of me with his arms crossed looking down. Slightly shorter than six feet tall, he had gelled black hair with his clean shave and a wider stomach than he thought. Seconds and even thirds were more common in this household, and I was not sure if he thought his size made him manlier, but I always thought it might be unhealthy.

"Look, Neesha, we're not even going to discuss this. We distinctly told you it was time for bed! We came home last night and told all you kids to go to bed. There's not a question in what you were supposed to be doing. We said it was time for bed! What the hell were you thinking? Why would you think it was okay to do whatever you wanted!" he yelled, as I looked away. "You disobeyed me. You can't seriously be blaming Will."

"But I didn't—" I tried to say before he interrupted me.

"No, I don't care what you did or did not do. You decided to go out there. We heard you walking out of Anita's room last night. We heard you! Don't pretend like they did this. This is your fault, Neesha. All of it!"

That was the moment when I started to blame myself for everything that happened on New Year's Eve.

Every single thing.

3 ∘ *no hugs*
sunday, january 1, 2006

After leaving my uncle's room, I had no desire to even glance in anyone's direction, especially that of Mark or Will. I sat back on the couch and stared out the window, noticing Will's car was not in the driveway anymore. I knew he must have told Rob before he left, and I assumed Anita probably found out too. Letting out a sigh of relief, at least Will was gone, but as I turned to the doorway, I saw Mark looking in my direction. Then he took a step toward me.

Was he serious?

He held out his arms like Santa and waited for me to stand up to hug him as if we were friends after that night—as if I had any trust left in him. I couldn't think of a reason why he would even want to see me. Everything was wrong, and he thought we could just hug and make up? I kept avoiding eye contact as he walked closer to me as if we were going to have normal chitchat like we used to. Inside I was fuming, and I wished I could scream at the top of my lungs.

I finally looked him straight in the eyes. Astonished to see him smiling, I shook my head. "What do you want?" I asked.

"Come on, don't be like that," he said.

"Oh, please..." I rolled my eyes.

"Neesha, you're leaving today. I wanted to say goodbye."

Why the hell would he want to talk to me? I despised everything about him now. He used to be a friend I looked up to. We had been playing basketball and going to family events together for years. He could go to hell for all I cared.

"Bye."

"Come on, you've known me forever. Give me a hug goodbye."

I sat there and stared at him. I tried to convey as much of a tough attitude as I could while breaking down inside, but the most I could do was stare. The look in his eyes was so much like it had been the night before, and it made me shiver.

Clinging to my wet tissue, I stood up, my hands cupped together over my mouth. My right foot followed my left toward him, and he hugged me. I kept my arms as close to my body as possible as he squeezed me against him. But as soon as his arms loosened, I backed away as fast as I could and dashed out of the room.

My heart fell to the pit of my stomach as I walked briskly into Anita's room to pack my suitcase. Why was Mark acting like nothing happened the night before?

Then my mind jumped. What would my parents say when I returned home? Would I act like nothing happened as well? I was going to be in so much trouble.

After all, it was entirely my fault. Everyone said so.

I finished packing and headed toward the stairs. Feeling like I would be racing in the Olympics, I was so nervous I could barely breathe. I dreaded those stairs because I knew when I took my last step at the bottom, I would see my aunt and uncle again.

I held my breath as I walked into the kitchen expecting to see everyone upset with me. I grumbled a "hello" but that was about it. My eyes were bloodshot, my face was puffy, and everyone knew I didn't want to be there. How could I pretend like everything was okay when nothing was okay?

I waited for one of them to say something, but my aunt ignored me as she bustled about the kitchen. My uncle did the same, sitting across from me at the kitchen table. Wanting to push him into the pool or off a building, I had never felt this type of rage toward him. I didn't want to be related to him anymore. He was no family of mine.

"I'm going to call your mom," he said at last.

My heart sank. I moved to one of their high-top stools as he made the phone call. Was he going to tell her what happened last night? Avoiding eye contact, I told my aunt that I wasn't hungry when she handed me a bowl of cereal. My uncle began talking to my mom on speakerphone, but he didn't mention anything about Will or Mark.

"Say 'hi' to your mom, Neesha," he told me. His tone was friendly, but his glance was firm.

"Hi, Mom."

"How was your night?" she asked.

It was the worst night of my life. "It was good."

"Are you excited to head up to Dallas today?"

"Yeah."

"Well, your dad and I miss you, babe. I am glad you had a good New Year's. I know it's your favorite holiday. Would you say it was the best so far since you got to stay with Rob and Anita?"

"Yeah, sure. I miss you too, Mom. We'll have to talk later. I love you."

"I love you too. Have a safe trip, and call me tomorrow."

I hung up, handed the phone back to my uncle, and walked away.

4 ∘ *one more day*

To celebrate New Year's Day 2006, my cousins, uncle, and I were scheduled to head up to Dallas for their long-awaited football game. I had been excited, but now it was all meaningless to me. I stared at my silver phone in my lap, hoping the message light would blink so I could respond. Eager to hear from Jane, Emma, or Brad, I just wanted to get my mind off all this.

"Let's go, people," I mumbled to myself as I waited by the front door for my uncle and cousins. My aunt came to see us off, and I forced the word *goodbye* out of my mouth.

This would be the last word I would ever say to her again.

As I walked out of the house in Houston, I could feel a frozen wind engulf me and carry me off into a void. I was leaving the terrible events of that night behind in the exercise room, but I was headed into the bitter unknown with the memories of everything that happened. My breathing slowed out of nervousness—not the terror I had felt the night before, but rather a conscious fear, like what a dancer feels when she is walking into a ballet audition. My body felt distant as I jumped into the back of the black Escalade. I wished I had enough battery power on my iPod to listen to it on the drive.

"I'm so excited for the game!" Anita shouted to my uncle and Rob. "Can you change the song though? We've heard this one a million times."

"Shut up, Anita. This is a great song, plus I'm riding shotgun, so I get to play whatever music I want," Rob said.

The drive to Dallas lasted a few hours, but it felt like years as I sat deadened in the backseat. Wondering why Anita and Rob hadn't asked if I was okay, I just tried to ignore them.

I finally gave in and texted Jane. *Hey, what's up? I really need to talk when you have a chance.*

She responded, *Hi! I got your message, but I'm with my family right now. Are you okay?*

Not really, but I am with Anita and Rob and just need to get out of here.

Don't you guys have that football game, what's going on? Can you text me what happened. I can't talk till later.

I would rather just tell you when we talk. It's kind of a crazy story.

All right. I'll be around in a few hours. Talk to ya then!

OK, I typed.

I wanted to get it out of the way now instead of carrying this around with just me knowing. Jane had been my friend for years, and I knew that my best friends would always take my side. For some reason, I felt safest reaching out to Jane about everything. Even though I had always told everything to Emma, who knew me better than anyone, I just didn't know what she would say. I knew she wouldn't know how to respond. How could anyone? I wished I could tell Emma, but fear still overwhelmed me. She would never judge me, but I just felt ashamed of myself and didn't want to put the weight of that on her.

I had known Jane for years, and we were always close even though we weren't very similar. She played soccer and had two little brothers she went snowboarding and camping with all the time. A tomboy with blonde hair and blue eyes, Jane was taller than most of the girls at school and better in every sport than all the boys. She wore sweatpants and T-shirts most of the time and occasionally a hoodie from one of her soccer camps. We could relate on a sports level, but she always made fun of me because I played the "girliest" sport. I guess I did, but I never could have played contact sports. Way too aggressive. We had the same sense of humor, and she would always be sitting in the front row of the bleachers during my volleyball games. I would be on the field in my spandex shorts and red T-shirt after my practice ended to support her soccer team, with a cotton candy–flavored snow cone in hand.

A couple of hours later, my family and I checked into the Hyatt downtown in Dallas, then we took the elevator up to our suite on the fourth floor. Rushing past Rob when he opened the door, I grunted a halfhearted apology and ran into the bathroom to call Jane. It was a surprisingly big bathroom for a hotel room. I paced five steps back and forth about seven times before I finally sat on the side of the bathtub.

"Deep breaths," I muttered to myself until she finally answered.

"Hey Neesha, sorry it took so long for me to answer. We were just finishing up eating."

"It's fine, I'm just kind of freaking out."

"What's going on? What happened last night? Are you okay?"

"Look, essentially we all were just watching a movie and drinking a little champagne and having fun. I was with Anita most of the night, just talking about how Will was so cute and how I might have like a little crush on him."

"Wait, who's Will again? You met him recently right? Rob's friend?"

"I met him at Thanksgiving. He and Mark are friends, but I seriously have met him once before this party. I don't know him at all. I had no idea he was going to be here till like a day before New Year's Eve. I'm freaking out, Jane. I can't believe this happened."

"What happened? Seriously, what is going on?"

"I mean, basically I left Anita's room really late when my aunt and uncle told everyone to go to bed, and then we all did. But Mark and Will were in the same room where we watched the movie, and I wanted to know what they were doing. I couldn't sleep, and the room was close to Anita's, so then I left to say hi and see if they were still awake. I don't know why I did it. I don't know why I left. I just wanted to see Will. I couldn't stop myself from going out there."

"Okay, then what happened?"

"I literally don't even know. He led me to the exercise room, and like a million things happened, and I can barely remember. But Jane... I...I don't even know."

"What, Neesha? You can tell me anything. What happened?"

"I mean, Will made me..." I went silent.

"He made you what?"

"He made me give him head." I started to choke up as the words came out.

"Oh my god, Neesha. Oh my god. Where was Mark?"

"Jane, I can barely do this right now. I can't even tell you. I don't even know what to say or what happened or what is going to happen. I'm panicking," I tried to say through my short breaths.

"Where was he? You can tell me. I know this is so hard and I am so sorry, but you know you can trust me."

"I know, he was like, he was basically...there was this blanket, and he started to finger me, and I mean I don't even know why he would do that. I can't even think about either of them. I want to throw up..."

"Oh my god," she said gasping when I told her that it wasn't just Will, but someone else was involved. Someone who was supposed to be my friend.

"I don't know what to do. My aunt and uncle don't believe me, and Will turned the whole situation on me—everyone did."

"What about Anita and Rob?"

"They have said nothing to me. I am so fucking mad at them I don't even know what to say. I can barely look at any of these people, and my aunt was such a bitch. I can't stand her. She did not believe anything I said, which is ridiculous! I can't even believe this is happening. My mom is going to kill me. Like, I'm so screwed."

"Neesha, one second. Slow down. This is not your fault, and let me just tell you I am so beyond sorry that this happened to you, and please know that I love you so much, and I wish I could take all of this away. You are going to be fine, and I know this is terrible, but you can't kill yourself over this. You're going to just have to tell your mom."

Why would I kill myself? "Jane, no, no, no. I can't."

"You have to! You have to tell her the truth, or this is going to be a mess. You're going to have to tell her before your uncle does."

"I can't. I won't. I can barely even have this conversation right now, I'm so..." I began to sob quietly to myself.

"Are you okay? Neesha? I'm here for you no matter what you need. I love you so much. I'm so sorry."

"I'm fine, thanks. I am. I love you too. I really...I just have to go. I'll talk to you later."

As I relived the night for her, I began to finally understand that what happened to me was worse than I thought. Hearing the horrified, sympathetic reaction of one of my best friends, I considered for a second that maybe—just maybe—the night wasn't my fault.

When I hung up the phone, I could hear the sound of *Top Chef* on Bravo. My cousins and uncle must have been watching it in the suite's living room. I bit my nails as short as they would go before bleeding. I tasted little bits of skin, which was the only thing I had eaten all day. I wanted coffee or a Diet Coke, but I couldn't get rid of the feeling I had. Something just felt off. I felt shaky and kept getting the chills. I would be perfectly warm one second—almost hot—and then get a rush of an ice-cold wind. Sitting on the white toilet bowl now, my cold body no longer felt young. Numbly I realized that my childhood was further from me than I had ever imagined it could be. Pain shot through my eyes as I ran my hands through my hair. The black holes I saw as my eyes pressed against my knees could have swallowed up anyone.

The white towels hanging on the wall and the little soaps next to the sink—they all felt far from me. The blue soap stayed in the white seashell dish; it wouldn't make me clean. Still, I stared at the soaps for twenty minutes, deciding if I should take a shower.

"Just let me go home. Just let me get the hell out of here," I mumbled to myself.

I decided to take a quick shower to try and clean my dirty body and finally came out of the bathroom to get different clothes to change into. I grabbed a hoodie, from a volleyball camp I went to with Emma two summers before, and a different pair of dark jeans. I changed into this outfit, although I didn't want to be in anything tight fitting. Trying to stretch out my jeans, which were a size double zero, they felt too tight. Letting out a huge sigh, I knew I had to go to dinner with my family before the game.

My cousins, uncle, and I headed down to the lobby, where we ate together at the restaurant. A silent elevator ride preceded a volatile dinner. I ordered plain pasta with red sauce and a Diet Coke. My uncle had a steak, while Anita and Rob both got burgers. Everyone knew the tension was there, but no one would address it.

"Neesha, why aren't you eating?" my uncle finally asked me. "You haven't eaten anything all day, and you know my rule—you have to eat all your food before we can go."

"I'm really not hungry or in the mood," I told him while sipping my Diet Coke. I rolled my eyes in frustration. "And I don't want to go to the game either. I feel—I feel…I just really don't want to go, and like I'm sorry, but I'm not in the mood to be here. You guys should just go to the game without me."

"No, we want you to come," Anita told me with a look of sadness.

I turned in Rob's direction, but he wouldn't even look at me. I couldn't figure out why he could possibly be mad. I squinted at him before losing my cool.

"Thanks Anita, you're being really nice, but I think you might be the only one who wants me to come. I am not doing this anymore. I don't want to be at this dinner. I'm going back to the room."

"Neesha, you are being ridiculous. Finish your dinner. You don't have to go to the game, but you're going to finish your dinner," my uncle said.

"No, I won't. I am going upstairs."

My uncle let me leave while they finished dinner and then went to the game. I scurried up to the room and changed back into my pajamas but kept my sweatshirt on. Exhausted, having barely slept for a couple of days, I fell right to sleep. When everyone returned from the game, they brought little ice cream cups, including my favorite: chocolate chip cookie dough. Anita came over to me and asked, "Hey, are you okay? I brought you your favorite ice cream. Do you want any?"

"Thanks, that's really sweet, but I'm not hungry."

"Well, you should probably eat something. Do you want something else?"

How about you standing up to your parents and taking my side? How about saying something to your brother? Or saying something to your brother's stupid fucking friends? How about knowing that I didn't do anything wrong and defending me? "I'm fine. But I think I'm going to go back to sleep."

"Okay, but let me know if—"

"Just, like, drop it. There's really nothing you could say at this point. I honestly don't want to talk. I just want to sleep."

Anita left the room and closed the door quietly. I fell back asleep as soon as she left. The next morning I woke up empty. Shuffling around the suite, I brushed my teeth and tasted the mint toothpaste in a way I never had before. It almost made me nauseous. Wanting to throw up, I couldn't even finish brushing my teeth. Packing up quietly, I walked outside into the living room. Anita and Rob were sitting on the couch packing their things.

"Hey, how's it going?" Anita asked with a half smile.

"Do you know when we're leaving?"

"No, but I think soon. My dad's just finishing getting ready."

I took a seat next to Anita on the couch and stared at the TV. Glancing at my phone to see if anyone had texted me, I looked up to see my uncle in the doorway of his room. I immediately avoided eye contact and stared at the ground.

"Are you guys all ready? We're heading out in fifteen," my uncle said.

"Yep," my cousins responded together. I nodded and gave a fake, exaggerated smile with no teeth.

We headed down to the lobby to check out before having lunch on the way to the airport. That lunch was the last meal I would eat for a while.

We went to Hooter's. I couldn't figure out who actually ate at that restaurant. I had never set foot in it before. I ended up shuffling in with the rest of my family and sitting at a big booth. Chicken wings, of all things. Everyone ordered an excessive amount of wings while I ordered Diet Coke and said I would just share the wings. I ended up eating six, almost seven before realizing I should probably stop. And I didn't even like chicken.

My uncle chimed in, "Neesha, are you not going to eat again? What's the problem? You've barely eaten anything."

"Dad, just leave her alone," Anita interrupted.

Silently I kept eating my chicken wings with a mild hot sauce as I licked my lips, tasting every last drop of sauce. I liked the sauce. I just didn't like the wings. Eventually, I had them refill my glass twice before realizing it wouldn't be the best idea for my bladder on the plane. I had the smallest bladder in the world. So did my dad. We always joked about it as I grew up because we would need to stop the same amount of times on road trips to volleyball tournaments and long car rides to the hotel in Hawaii.

Once we headed to the airport, I felt a sense of relief even though I was sitting with Rob in the backseat. Listening to my iPod, I tried to ignore the fact that he hadn't really asked me anything about what was going on or apologized for anything—whether it was his conniving friends or that he never asked me if I was okay or for not taking my side. At least Anita tried to be there for me, but Rob did nothing. He hadn't said anything to me, and I couldn't believe that they didn't try to stand up to their parents for me.

We arrived at the Dallas airport, and it was finally time for me to get out of this place. Swinging the car door open, I raced into the airport without thinking twice about how fast anyone else was coming. I ended up beating everyone inside, tapping my black tennis shoe on the floor. I faked a smile as silence fell, then I forced myself to hug Rob and Anita.

"Have a safe trip home. Good to see you," Anita said.

"Thanks," I said even though I didn't really mean it. Rob didn't say anything besides a halfhearted "bye" as he hugged me. I wanted nothing to do with them anymore, but I held an ounce of hope that maybe one day they would take my side against Will and Mark.

My cousins had never really seen a cold side to me. I had always been the upbeat, peppy young girl with a bit of an attitude, but I just couldn't be her anymore. They could see my smile had faded and how on edge I was feeling. In only a matter of days, their sometimes-shy-around-boys-and-always-a-little-awkward cousin had turned into someone they didn't know anymore.

I could tell that the goodbye with Anita felt withdrawn, which it never was before. She had been the sister to me that I always wished I had. We used to talk on the phone at least twice a week ever since we both got our first cell phones. She always understood me, and we knew everything about each other. We had never even fought before, and we always took each other's side. I could tell her anything, but now I didn't even want to look at her. They were my favorite part of my family, but that halfhearted goodbye and "good to see you" would be the last words I would ever hear from them again.

A few steps away from us, my uncle looked at me with a disappointed frown. My eyes were hollow and empty. I swallowed whatever saliva was in my mouth from lunch as my stomach sank. Then I took a step toward him.

"Look, you're probably wondering if I'm going to tell your mom what you did, but I don't know yet. I don't know what to tell her," he said.

Hearing those words, I wished I had felt something, but there was no feeling left in me for this man who had been so appalling and unsupportive. I only blamed him for not taking my side and not even giving me the benefit of the doubt. I never wanted to see him again. Ever.

He opened up his arms similar to the way Mark did the morning before, but did he really think I would possibly hug him? I turned around as fast as I could, but the effort it took exhausted me, and my steps away from my family felt like those of a sloth. I placed one foot in front of the other, feeling like I could barely move.

My flight back home to New Mexico could not come soon enough. I needed to be out of that entire state, and I needed to be out of a place filled with a bunch of people who refused to believe someone in their own family. My uncle's betrayal hurt most of all. He had always been there for me, my entire life. He was my mother's younger brother. Her only brother. Didn't he have to support me in this? Didn't he have to support *her* in this? I thought I was a priority in his life.

I had thought wrong.

I put my suitcase on the security check's conveyor belt and walked through the metal detector without a backward glance. For the first time in my life, my family didn't feel like my family. Rob and Anita seemed like strangers, not even friends or acquaintances. We had grown up together. We'd celebrated every Thanksgiving together and some years even Diwali, the Indian Christmas. They were the only reason I ever felt like the Indian culture was a part of me. Back in Albuquerque, I never celebrated anything like that. In fact, I never really cared much for Indian food in general. I could never handle the spices. But my family made the tradition fun. I always looked forward to the annual Diwali celebration in Houston with dancing, family, and friends.

They understood me and accepted me as family even though I was adopted. They never made me feel like I was anything but the cousin that they loved so dearly. I never once questioned being a part of this family, and until now I never had a reason to.

My aunt and uncle had always treated me like one of their children, and I always looked up to them. Growing up, I thought my aunt was one of the most gorgeous people I'd ever seen, but now I couldn't think of one beautiful thing about her. My uncle was just like another parent to me. He always took me shopping with Anita, and we always received the same exact presents—after all, our birthdays were two weeks apart. Most of all, this part of my family never judged a single thing about me or made me feel like I wasn't good enough or pretty enough or anything like that. I could talk to all of them about anything, even things I didn't want to talk to my parents about. Whether it was boys or even frustration with my parents, they were always there for me.

But how could family turn so quickly against each other? I couldn't understand how Rob and Anita's bond with Will and Mark could be more important than their bond with me. I thought that they had to be faithful to me. I had no reason to think otherwise. I thought our family stuck together. I thought that my uncle would ask at least once if I was even okay. I couldn't understand why he never asked that, why my aunt or even my cousins never did either. Wasn't it a sensible question, making sure I was okay?

I grabbed my suitcase on the other side of the security checkpoint and didn't even bother wiping my eyes. I began shuffling to Gate B10 for my flight back to Albuquerque.

I was done with Texas.

5 ○ *in the air*
monday, january 2, 2006

That early afternoon flight from Dallas, Texas, to my home in Albuquerque, New Mexico, was the worst two hours imaginable—not because I was sitting next to some horrible, hacking old man or a screaming baby. It was because I could not stop thinking about that night. For the first time, I had no fear of flying; I had no desire to come down. The unknown felt so much worse than fear, but as I tried to distract myself in the plane, I realized this feeling was not about to go away. My mind drifted to my yearly spring break trips with my parents. We would fly to Hawaii, usually Maui, for a week of sunshine and virgin piña coladas, but I always knew I would have to make it through the terror that filled my body during every flight. Sitting in between my parents made me feel safer but could not entirely shake the apprehension that always seemed to come over me.

But this time, I was not sitting with my parents. I was by myself. Realizing I was in this situation alone, I knew I would have to deal with it by myself. My thoughts slowly came back to Houston, and my mind ran in circles, around and around, back and forth like someone deciding their punishment between a day without water or a day without food. I bit my chapped lips as if my teeth were rubbing against splintered wood, but I did not even notice.

I sat in the window seat beside an elderly woman who smelled like old newspaper and Chanel Number 5. Somewhere in her midsixties, she wore a short long-sleeve black dress over white tights. Her narrow thighs did not touch, even though her shiny black shoes clicked together on the airplane's beaten-up carpet. I glanced in her direction for a few seconds out of the corner of my eye and saw her staring down at her wrinkled hands in her lap. She turned to me with the kind of look you would give a baby in the grocery store who stared at you, and then she smiled. That smile forced my big brown eyes to close, eyes that must have been completely vacant. I finally opened them and forced a smile before my gaze bolted to the window again.

She put her hand on my leg and softly asked, "Are you okay, honey?"

Of course I'm not okay. I can't even breathe. "Yeah, thank you."

I dropped my eyes to the book I held in my wobbly hands—*Breakfast at Tiffany's.* Thirty thousand feet in the air, I began to shake my right foot uncontrollably while my thighs flinched back and forth. As I repeatedly crossed and uncrossed my legs, I read Capote's words about the "mean reds:", *You're afraid and you sweat like hell, but you don't know what you're afraid of.*

As if my fear of flying wasn't bad enough, I couldn't even distract my mind by reading this novel. A two-hour flight felt like eternity, yet I had no desire for it to end. I had convinced myself to the point of terror that I was in serious trouble with my parents for letting this happen. Putting my long hair up in a ponytail gave me a second to notice the tray table in front of me, but it just made me feel like I couldn't move. As my hair fell back into my face, I gave up in a huff and placed my pink hair tie back on my wrist. Drumming my fingers one at a time in order across my book, my mind ran away from me.

It ran to the darkest corner where no one ever wants to be. The corner of your childhood mind in the middle of a nightmare that makes you want to jump into your parents' bed and never leave. The part of the nightmare that forces your body into shock, and all of a sudden your eyes bolt open, waking you up. When you're screaming in your dream and you can't stop, no matter what you do to try, you just can't. The part where life seems closer to death when you are running away from the bad guy and he has you pinned up against a wall in the corner of a dark alley. All the effort in the world won't make the good guy appear, the one who's supposed to save you. The corner where there's no sunlight and there's no heaven, just a permanent hell.

As my thoughts bounced in and out of the shadows, a soft teardrop fell onto my book to dampen the page. What would have happened if they just believed me? If I had the chance to explain my side of this story and my family gave me a hug and asked me if I was okay, would I be? How did I lose the trust of my aunt and uncle so fast? What did I do wrong? I was just like one of their kids all of these years, but now…

Disgust built up for my family in Houston, as well as for Will and Mark. But most of all, I disgusted myself. My legs felt detached from my body. The only thing I had left was my mind, which I could barely keep track of. It felt restless and forced every finger of mine to twitch. Biting my fingernails as my hot pink nail polish chipped off, I no longer had the top whites on my nails. Only wet skin that was now red and raw remained.

I closed my eyes, but I was left with the image of the exercise room. I shook my head rapidly four times. I could not get rid of that white exercise room.

I wasn't raped, I repeated in my head over and over, to make it okay. I wasn't raped.

I wasn't raped.

I wasn't raped.

I wasn't raped.

I wasn't raped.

I wasn't raped.

I thought that if I could remove myself from the catastrophe and pretend like nothing happened, my parents would never know. If I acted like nothing happened, then nothing did happen. If I could pretend like I was the same person that I was the week before, then I was. I could have the freedom of being the carefree girl I used to be if I really believed I could.

I closed my eyes again, and a specific day in the third grade came to mind. I remembered one of the few days when I felt almost as sad as I did now. Not because I was the only one in the class who was not invited to Jane's birthday party, but because I could not stop hearing about it. Everyone in the class was excited about the birthday party at the water park on a Saturday in April. While we were learning to write our names in cursive, I kept to myself and listened to the whispers about the party. But the unhappiest part was when all the kids surrounded her during recess. Just like every other girl, I wanted to fit in and be just like Jane, but I wasn't.

I spent that recess sitting by myself on one of the metal swings by the library, humming songs and brushing my white tennis shoes in the dirt, not really knowing why I felt so upset that I needed to be alone. This wasn't my normal behavior. I had always been a people person. I supposed that was the only way for me to let things go and move forward. Maybe I did need more time by myself.

As I looked out the window of the plane, I saw that nine-year-old girl. She was sitting on the black swing in blue leggings and a white sweatshirt. I remembered how all I wanted was to get out of that place as I rocked back and forth on the swing. I did not feel strong at all when I isolated myself in elementary school, and I rarely spent time alone. Whenever I did feel the need to run away from whatever troubled me at the time, I only felt neglected and lonely. I never learned to enjoy my solitude, not even now. I associated being alone with being sad, which felt all too appropriate in this plane.

That bottomless feeling resonated with my current misery, but I told myself that I had to be strong this time around. At all of fourteen instead of nine, there was no longer room for weakness. Maybe I needed to learn to be okay with dealing with something on my own. After all, I could not think of who would really help me let go of what just happened in Houston. I was not that weak little girl in elementary school anymore. What happened then was not what had just happened, and I couldn't pretend like these were the same feelings. I knew that now I would be stronger. I had to be.

6 ∘ *no place like home*

When I arrived at the Albuquerque airport, I couldn't fathom seeing my parents. Did my uncle tell them what happened while I was on the plane? Did they believe him? Were they angry? How much trouble was I in?

My parents were waiting for me just past the security checkpoint, open-armed and elated to see me. I bit my dry lip as they hugged me— the first loving embrace I received since that night.

"How was the trip?" my mom asked as we headed to the parking lot.

I trailed through the airport between her and my dad, my eyes looking at the ground. My body felt heavier than ever before. I put on another sweatshirt as we walked outside. I shook ever so slightly as I tried to fake a smile.

I lied. "Good."

"Yeah?" My mom took my face in her hand and turned it toward her. "Are you okay? You don't look like you feel so well."

I pushed her hand away. "I'm just tired and really want to go to bed." With a forced smile, I tried to change the topic. "But I'm looking forward to going back to school tomorrow. It will be nice to see Jane, Emma, and Brad."

"How were their holiday breaks? Have you talked to them?" my mom asked.

"I'm sure they are all fine. I talked to Jane a little. I know she was with her family."

"How are her parents doing? I haven't seen them in a while."

"They're good. She spent the holiday with them and her little brothers. I think they went skiing or something."

"And Emma and Brad?" my dad chimed in.

I tried to keep my usual lively voice even though the incessant questioning made my mind race. "They spent New Year's together. They were both in Albuquerque."

"Was Emma's sister in town?"

"I know she was here for Christmas. I'm not sure if she went back to the East Coast yet or not. I think everyone is doing pretty well. Christmas break is a little weird not seeing everyone for a few weeks."

"Well, you'll see them all tomorrow. Did you and Anita get to play any volleyball while you were visiting? Tell us more about the trip," my dad said.

"I mean, not really. We went to her school one day. It has one of the nicest gyms I've ever seen."

"I can imagine."

"But no, we really just spent time at home and with Rob's friends. We went out to eat a lot, and we went to that one super fancy restaurant one night. The one we always go to. We did some shopping—basically the usual things we do…" My voice tapered off.

"That sounds like fun. Well, I'm sure it will be good to get back to see your friends at school."

But I didn't know what Brad and Emma would say. I thought I would be tainting their perfect childhood lives if I told them what happened. Brad was the boy who could make me laugh no matter what. He was the theater star, landing a lead role every year. He was the only boy I ever really trusted and the one closest to me. He wore Gap from head to toe, white Converse tennis shoes, Lacoste tees, and designer jeans. He looked older than everyone else, and he would be the first to tell me how pretty I was. I never questioned our friendship. Genuine, very sure of himself, confident, and poised, he was someone I admired. Blond hair and blue eyes just like Jane. We constantly teased them about how they could be brother and sister. He was taller than Jane, thin and lanky, and I always knew he would be an actor—ego, enthusiasm, personality, and drive included.

If he taught me anything it was to be bold and brave. His courage was inspiring, and he didn't give a care in the world about what people thought about him. I wished I didn't either. He had one younger sister, whom we never really spent too much time with, but his parents were great. I loved his mom dearly and looked forward to seeing her when I went over to their house. Brad made me feel like everything would always be okay. He had a calming tone in his voice. I could not wait to see him.

Even though Jane and Brad knew me just as well as Emma, Emma was different. She was my absolute best friend—the friend everyone wanted—and we had a friendship that could never be broken. Whether we were eating breakfast burritos in the morning at school, gossiping in the back of English class, or just painting our nails at her house, we had the best time. She started playing volleyball too but never took it as seriously as I did. I never had a friendship like this before because I had not met a a person who truly understood me with a look. I didn't have to say anything for her to know what I was thinking. She was the type of friend I hoped everyone found one day. Emma always knew if I was hiding something, so I was a little nervous to see her.

Once in my mom's silver Lexus, I let out a quiet sigh of relief. The weather felt much colder than I remembered when I left for Houston, but I didn't mind. There was something about feeling cold when I was already numb that no longer bothered me. Staring out the window, I crossed my legs anxiously and tapped my foot up and down—similar to what I did in the plane. My parents seemed to notice I wasn't feeling conversational. They left me alone on the ride home, isolated with my awful thoughts. I thought about what I would say when I saw my friends the next day at school, but I mainly focused on how to clear my mind of everything that just happened.

When we arrived home, I staggered to my room with my suitcase and began unpacking. I took out a pink tank top that I had bought in Houston, before New Year's, from Abercrombie—the one for kids. The size was a medium, which should probably have fit a ten-year-old. I stared at this shirt, now realizing that it was too small for me. The shirt matched most of the clothes in my closet, a frilly collection of girly outfits perfect for the normal fourteen-year-old. But I wasn't that girl anymore.

Staring at my clothes, I realized I needed something to focus on, to distract myself from the constant flashbacks of those boys. That something would be disappearance—the disappearance of myself.

I tried the tank top on. Too small. I told myself that it would fit by the end of the week.

Soon after, I walked to the bathroom and took out the scale. The needle settled on 90 pounds. I was five foot two, petite and lean. That weight might have seemed small to some, but to me, in that moment, it didn't seem reasonable; it seemed too high. Standing on the scale, I was hit with insecurities. The number was terrifying.

Walking out of the bathroom, I went back to my room and looked around for a moment. It had never been so silent. Everything looked the same, but nothing felt the same. I was determined to make it go back to the way it was, focusing no longer on that night and instead on my weight.

But what about that night? I couldn't just make it go away. I tried to brace myself for the inevitable punishment I would receive from my parents and tensed my entire body just thinking of what frightening reaction they would have. After all, it was entirely my fault. I might have been family, but everyone in Houston already blamed me. I couldn't possibly stand up to my parents after what just happened. My mom and dad would surely take their side.

I lay on my floor, which would soon become an all too familiar pastime. I brought my laptop down from my desk and started to browse the Internet a bit—a few of the usual social media sites that were popular, like MySpace and LiveJournal. I also browsed websites about volleyball or fashion sites like *Vanity Fair* or *Teen Vogue*.

KNOCK KNOCK.

"Neesha!" my mom called.

I jumped up and opened the door to find her standing in the hall. She smiled. No punishment yet, it seemed.

"I brought your favorite salad back from dinner earlier. We went to Scarpas before we picked you up from the airport. It's in the fridge whenever you're done unpacking."

Food? I can't even fit in my new shirt. "Thanks."

I closed the door and waited ten minutes before tiptoeing into the kitchen. I knew my parents would be upstairs in their room by then. I took the white Styrofoam box out of the fridge and set it on the colossal island in the middle of the kitchen. The island contained the stove with four different burners, a sizeable cutting board on the counter, and a hefty red bowl full of fresh fruit. Not bothering to turn on the TV, I stared at the salad in the box with absolutely no desire to eat it. The concept of a satisfying meal in my body just made me nauseous. I then considered what to do with the salad. I felt like it would be completely wasteful if I were to throw it all away, so I settled for licking the Greek dressing off of the green leaves. I thought a couple of calories that night wouldn't be the worst thing since I planned on eating nothing the next day to try and look like a kid again. If I could fit in my new shirt, everything would be okay.

Afterward, I dumped the rest of the salad in the disposal. Running the sink and watching the leaves go down the drain, I felt significantly stronger than anyone should after doing something so bizarre.

Everything would be all right if I was able to say no to something. It would give me the strength I lacked. I could be strong enough to fix this on my own and pretend like nothing happened.

I hid in my room for the rest of the night. I wanted an escape from myself, from the reality into which I had been thrown. For the first time in my life, I wanted to feel nothing and I wanted to be nothing.

7 ∘ *control yourself*
tuesday, january 3, 2006

I woke the next morning with a false sense of strength. The hunger in my belly made me feel the emptiness I was searching for. Since I was back home, back to what I knew, everything was fine. Nothing had changed. I was still the fragile girl I used to be before this horrific trip.

But that sense of strength vanished when I looked at myself in the mirror. My body felt divided and broken from my mind, like a shattered piece of glass on the floor. Those two boys had damaged it beyond repair. It had no beauty left in it, and I didn't think it deserved my respect anymore. The memory of their hands on my body and inside of me took away any ownership I had for myself.

I put on size double zero blue jeans and a beige T-shirt with a puffy white jacket from the Gap. That morning I didn't bother putting on any makeup to cover up how tired I looked with dark brown bags under my eyes. I didn't care. I braced myself for the morning as I pushed away my black eyeliner and bright pink blush.

I strolled into the kitchen before my dad drove me to school, and I whispered "morning" to my mom in a hoarse voice. I shook my right foot and thought about the dreadful three hours of sleep I might have gotten the night before.

"Morning, Neesha. How'd you sleep?"

Terrible and not at all. "Good, you?"

"I slept well. I made you a breakfast burrito for your ride to school. I put a little bit of mild green chili in it for you. I thought you might have missed it while you were in Texas, but it's not too spicy, I promise."

"Thanks, Mom."

"I made you coffee too. It's right there," she said pointing to my spot at the table.

I sat there watching my mom read the newspaper, in her white robe with purple flowers. She was your typical Indian mom: caring and strong. Just about an inch or two shorter than me, standing at five feet tall, with straight black hair that rested on her shoulders, she was nothing but warm and welcoming to everyone. Her family came first no matter what. Her family was Indian—her parents were born there—but she grew up in Zimbabwe. After she finished high school in Africa, she moved to Dallas to attend Southern Methodist University. When she moved to America, she met my dad the first semester of their freshman year at SMU.

My dad grew up in Cleveland, Ohio, and had spent his first four months out of high school working in Kenya, where he developed his love for anthropology. When he returned to Ohio, he interned at the Museum of Natural History and worked on the reconstruction of Lucy's skull, the 3.2-million-year-old skeleton of one of our earliest human ancestors, for *The New York Times* and *Newsweek*. He then pursued his studies in physical anthropology. Soon he met my mom in their co-ed dorm in the fall of 1978, and they connected on their time spent in Africa. Their mutual experiences linked them quickly, and they began dating about six months later.

As I drank my coffee at the table, my dad walked into the kitchen to greet my mom, and I thought about my parents' picture-perfect love that I hoped to have one day, distracting myself from why I was hiding from them about New Year's. I wished the memory would just go away and I could keep fantasying about my future and falling in love.

My parents met for the first time when they were walking back from the cafeteria to their dorm building. My dad walked up to my mom and asked how she was doing. She answered, "I hate this place. I hate everyone here. I hate everything!" Naturally he was taken aback. In her defense, my mom was eighteen, probably homesick, depressed, and lonely, and my dad caught her at a bad time. His response was something like "I'm sorry." They had reached their dorm by this time, and he simply said, "Okay, see you later."

Her room was on the second floor of the dorm, and at the end of the corridor, there was a window that looked out onto the lawn. She used to spend a lot of time sitting there, looking out the window daydreaming about her home in Zimbabwe. The next time my dad spoke to her, she was sitting by the window. From then on, they spent all their time together.

A few weeks later, they skipped their English class to see a movie for their first date. Their teacher knew them quite well because they never missed class. She noticed right away that they were both absent and made a comment like "Both Rohini and David are missing. Hmmm, I wonder what's going on."

My parents had been dating for about two weeks before he kissed her. Actually, he asked permission to kiss her first. Up until that time, they mainly talked, occasionally held hands, and simply got to know each other. My mom always told me how my dad was very supportive and protective of her—a true gentleman.

Growing up, I heard the best stories about their relationship. My dad, always very kind and loving with my mom, had a huge heart. As a foreign student, she had limited financial resources both because of her government at home and her dad. Her government would allow any money she needed for school tuition, books, living, but her dad was so against her coming to America that he would only send the necessary amount for tuition and books. Consequently, she didn't have money for meals on weekends, when the school cafeteria was closed. She always insisted on paying her own way through college, but when she didn't have enough money for food on Sunday nights, she would have cup of noodles soup in her room. My dad would join her, even though he left her room hungry many times.

Then my dad proposed a year later, in the fall of 1979. My dad's brother-in-law used to come to Dallas on business trips, and he had asked him to bring his grandmother's diamond ring with him. He then proposed to my mom in her dorm room, and their engagement was three-years long. In 1982, they had two ceremonies for their wedding: a Hindu ceremony in Dallas, where my mom wore an intricate gold-and-red wedding sari, and then a few weeks later, a Western ceremony at my grandparents' house in Ohio, where she wore a traditional white wedding dress.

After my dad received his master's degree, my parents moved to New Mexico, where my dad entered the PhD program in physical anthropology. Due to health reasons, my mom was unable to have children, but they knew they really wanted kids. My parents had close friends who had adopted internationally, and after an exhausting process, my parents finally adopted me from Calcutta, India, in 1991.

Even though she wasn't my biological mother, my mom was my closest friend and the best mom anyone could ask for. People always asked me what I thought about being adopted, but I really didn't think much of it. My parents had always been my parents—adopted or not—and I never thought they were anything less than that. I looked up to both of them and admired the relationship they had with each other. They had the perfect long-lasting love that I was supposed to eventually have, before everything in Houston happened.

I continued to sip my coffee and looked outside at the beautiful view of the Sandia Mountains in my backyard. I had lived in Albuquerque, New Mexico, my entire life with very few problems. Getting any new CD I wanted or going shopping on Saturday mornings with my mom—nothing ever felt difficult. I appreciated the quaint environment of Albuquerque, but I knew that I wanted to get out. I went to private schools for elementary and middle school and was now attending a private high school. I hated the small school with all of its drama, but I ultimately knew it was the best place for me since I wanted to attend a good college outside of New Mexico. My biggest problem would be on the volleyball team or mean girls not getting their way and complaining about it.

My school—a small private school—didn't really know much about boundaries though. Many of the teacher's kids were bullies! So middle school was a bit rough for all my friends. Emma was one of the people who was bullied by the mean girls, but she never let it get to her. No matter how much Brooke, the main bully of the school, made fun of Emma about frivolous things, Emma always let it go. I admired that about her. Brooke felt the need to send snotty texts to Emma about her family or tell her that some boy didn't like her. Occasionally I would be with Emma in class and she would tell me what happened with Brooke. I always wanted to put Brooke in her place for Emma, but she never let me. Her level-headed nature always impressed me. Even though catty drama happened, as it usually did, I couldn't complain since it was the worst thing in my carefree life. I was lucky to have it so easy and to have such loving parents, so I never thought twice about being adopted.

But as I looked back down at my coffee, I realized there was only so much daydreaming I could do in my living nightmare. Just like that I snapped back to the reality that what happened in Houston destroyed my future fairy tale. That morning, my mom didn't seem to notice that I was not myself. She was absorbed in her own thoughts, I guess—or maybe I was hiding mine too well. I fidgeted, thinking about letting out the whole story as I swallowed a hot sip, but fear kept my mouth shut.

That first day back at school, I did not eat a single thing. I drank six bottles of water and robotically attended classes. One bottle of water during every class, I would stare at the clock or begin to daydream. Before this, I had never eaten absolutely nothing in a day, but for some reason it felt so easy; it felt right. Avoiding the cafeteria during lunch, I went to the library to be alone. I browsed the Internet on one of the computers and listened to my iPod instead of spending my lunch with Jane, Brad, and Emma.

Brad texted me, *Hey, where are you? You coming to lunch?*

I'm in the library. I have some homework, but I'll see you later in class.

OK. We miss you!

I wanted that day to last forever just so I didn't have to go home, convinced that my mom would have talked to my uncle by then. Once lunch ended, I filled up my water bottle again and knew I would be running into my friends in my next class. I walked slowly, hoping to avoid them on the way. Jane appeared behind me and tapped me on the shoulder.

"Neesha, are you okay?"

"Yeah, I really just don't want to talk about it."

"I'm really sorry about everything that happened," she told me as she tried to hug me.

"I know, I know. But I honestly can't do this right now."

"Well, if you need me at all, you know I'm here, or Emma or Brad. We're all here. Have you told them anything about Houston?"

"No, I just really don't want to tell them, and I don't want everyone knowing about it. So please don't say anything."

"I won't. I promise."

And that was that. We silently walked into our English class, and I took my usual seat next to Emma.

Emma turned to the right to see me, jumped out of her seat, and gave me the biggest hug. "Neesha! How was Houston? How are your cousins and everyone?"

"It was fine. I'm happy to be back."

"Yeah, me too. Tell me more—any cute boys? Any exciting updates?"

"A bunch of stuff happened, yeah, but I really can't give you all the updates about it right now. I'm so happy to see you though. How was your break?" I asked as I tried to be my usual energetic self.

"It was great. Brad and I went to a party with a bunch of my sister's friends. Pretty low-key, but we had fun. I know New Year's is your favorite holiday though, so I'm glad you had a good trip," she said before the teacher walked to the front of the class.

Brad, walking in late, saw me and gave a quick wink. As he walked by my seat, he squeezed my shoulder. I faked a smile and looked down at my desk. My two back-to-back classes sped by as I sipped my water and stared at the chalkboard, zoning out.

But after class I knew I had to find Jane. The suspense was killing me. "Jane, I need to talk. I can't do this. I have no idea what's going to happen. My mom has no idea what happened in Houston, and I'm freaking out."

"You need to tell her," she said.

"But I can't even say it out loud. I—"

"I know Neesha, but she needs to know the truth and more importantly, this wasn't your fault. You really should tell her your side of the story before someone in Houston says something. Have you spoken to your cousins or anyone?"

"No, I haven't spoken to any of them. I refuse to talk to Anita or Rob; I have nothing to say to them. I never want to talk to them again. I just...oh my god, I don't even know."

"You don't think they would take your side?"

I wonder if they would have believed me. Maybe they did but were too scared of my aunt and uncle to stand up to them. "I mean they had their chance to defend me and they didn't. What's the point? Honestly, what can they possibly do?" I asked.

"If someone else tells your parents before you do, things are going to be a lot worse. This is seriously not some little thing. I know you're trying to brush it off, but you really can't do that."

"I know, but what can I even do? If my uncle tells my mom—what if she believes him? And then...I just can't say that stuff to my mom."

"You really need to say something sooner rather than later. You're not in the wrong. I know this is so bad, but you just have to talk to her."

Not a chance in hell. "Ughh, I know, I know. You're right."

"And let me know if you need anything at all tonight. Just do it as soon as you get home so you don't have to stress yourself out about it anymore."

"Ok, thanks," I said as she hugged me.

Walking to my dad's silver Toyota 4Runner to go home, I turned on my pink iPod like I usually did. My dad looked at me with a smile when I stepped into the car.

"How was your day?"

"It was fine." My voice, quieter than usual, sounded harsh, but he brushed off the fact that I didn't ask him how his was in return. Turning up the radio, he didn't bother trying to talk to me more.

The drive home felt quicker than usual, but I dreaded every moment, wishing I could put off what I knew I had to tell my mom when I got back home. We drove about seven minutes before I saw the Starbucks we stopped at every day after school or after volleyball practice. It was next to a smoothie place called Keva Juice, and I would usually switch off between the two depending on what I was in the mood for. My dad asked if I wanted to stop to get anything as I nodded without making eye contact.

We both went into Starbucks, and when my dad ordered a black coffee, I chimed in, "I'll have one too." I had never ordered black coffee before. He gave me a curious look and asked, "You don't want a Frappuccino or your Caramel Macchiato?"

"No, I'm trying something new, Dad."

Before I knew it we had driven home, and half my coffee was gone. I found myself walking into the kitchen while my dad went to his study, and soon I saw my mom's questioning eyes. Instantly, I could tell she knew something was wrong.

"Neesha, what happened in Houston?" she asked as I shuffled down the hall, my heart sinking. Her voice sounded on edge, and I could see the lines on her forehead as she raised her eyebrows. "I just got off the phone with your uncle."

Whatever he told her, I knew it was not the whole truth. I heard his accusatory voice in my head, blaming me for what had happened that night. It made my heart race and infuriated me.

"Neesha?" my mom asked, the urgency in her voice increasing. "What happened?"

Just tell her. "Nothing," I lied as I walked into my room and slammed the door.

Five minutes later, my mom's voice accompanied the pounding of her fist on my door. "Neesha, I really need to know what happened that night. Right now."

"Mom, I don't want to talk about it," I said, shaking my head. "I just, I just can't."

"I need to know. This is very serious. I need to know exactly what happened. Please, you can tell me anything. I won't be mad at you. Just tell me."

I had never been more embarrassed about anything before in my life. My whole body trembled, and my voice quivered as I answered her through the door. "Look, I told Jane that night, but I can't talk about it again, Mom. I really can't."

Her voice was unsteady now too. "What about Emma and Brad?"

"No, I just told Jane, but I don't want to talk about this anymore."

"Then I need Jane's number, if you won't tell me what happened."

I scribbled down her number on a piece of paper and slipped it underneath the door without a word.

Fifteen minutes later, she returned with a quiet knock on my door. This time, I let her in. My mom held me close as I tried to keep my emotions together. In a painful grip that could not be fought, I shed heavy tears that no fourteen-year-old should ever cry.

"I am so sorry this happened. Are you okay? I am so sorry," my mom whispered.

But I desperately wanted her to stop hugging me. "Yeah, it's fine," I said.

It wasn't fine. She knew that, and so did I. I felt terrible that I was putting her through this, mortified that she now knew all the disgusting sexual things that had happened to me, to her only daughter. I began to feel dirty and gross, but I mostly felt violated again. I had already put a wall up between all the details of that night and myself. They were details I never wanted anyone to know about, ever. Especially not my mother. I just wanted them to stay in the past.

8 ○ *silence*

My perfect, innocent world felt farther away from me than ever. It was now in the past, and my childlike self was gone. My mother knew all my secrets, and I couldn't believe it. I tried to take a step back as I finally stopped crying, and my mom pulled away to look at me.

"Neesha, are you okay?" she asked me with the most heartbreaking look in her eyes that I had ever seen.

I could not believe that I had made my mom this miserable. Before this, I could count the amount of times I had seen her cry on one hand. I hurt my innocent mother, who had done nothing but let her daughter go visit her trusted family.

But even in the midst of my guilt, I thought, Are you kidding? Why on earth would I ever want to discuss this with you? Why would I want to discuss this with anyone? I didn't even want her to ask if I was okay. I wasn't and I didn't want to talk about it.

Turning my head away, I sat on my bed shaking my head, frozen. She finally left with tears in her eyes, walking down the hall to the kitchen. I heard her unsteady voice as she talked on the phone to her only brother.

Six minutes passed while I listened to her, but I couldn't make out her aggravated words. I snuck out of my room as quietly as possible and tiptoed down the hall. Hearing only bits of my mom's voice, I continued into the kitchen. As I sat on the wooden chair by the island, part of me felt an obligation to hear the phone call that had everything to do with me. Hatred and remorse overwhelmed me—hatred for my uncle but remorse for the fact that my mother's relationship with her brother was about to end. I watched my mom and listened to her carefully.

She looked at me before she spoke what would be her last words to her brother. I looked away, unable to meet her gaze.

"I trusted you. I...I..." she said as she tried to get the words out, but fury overtook her. "I trusted you with my daughter, and I trusted you to take care of her and put her first. And I can't talk to you right now because I have to make sure that my daughter is okay." She hung up the phone, and in that moment, her world shattered. There were hopeless tears in her eyes, and I knew she was crushed. She was crumbling, and I wasn't helping—how could I? I was damaged enough as it was.

Suddenly she threw the phone down on the kitchen counter. It crashed to the floor and broke into several pieces. Jumping in shock, my heart started to beat faster. It wasn't just the phone breaking—it was my mother's heart breaking, our family breaking.

Her heart was breaking for me.

That hurt the most.

My heart was broken too, but the pieces were on the floor of my uncle's exercise room in Houston. My heart had been left with members of my family who didn't care to take my side. It was left with the two boys who didn't care. No one cared in Texas. Will and Mark were probably joking about it right then.

What were they thinking? I considered for a second, before shaking my head to get them out of my mind. Sitting in the wooden seat in my kitchen, I played scenarios over and over about what was going on in my aunt and uncle's house after he hung up the phone. I wondered what lies my uncle was going to tell Rob and Anita, what lies he was going to tell my aunt. But the idea of seeing them or hearing any of their voices made me cringe as I shook the thoughts away.

I knew it killed my mother when she hung up the phone. She and her brother had been through so much together, and he was spitting on their relationship. Nothing could have hurt her more.

I desperately wanted that emotional moment when my mother and I would know that, through it all, we had each other. I wanted to give my mom a hug, to have that moment in the movies when a mother and daughter embrace and cry together. I thought that was what that next moment was going to be because we so badly needed each other. She needed to know that I would make it back from that night. She needed to know that I wouldn't hurt and that her fourteen-year-old daughter would be able to live happily after this. She needed to know that I was okay or was going to be eventually.

But I wasn't. And wouldn't be.

That moment didn't happen, because I couldn't find it in myself to get up and give her the hug she needed. I couldn't find the compassion that she needed. I couldn't find the love; it was missing. I had no love in my body at all. I didn't love myself anymore, so I couldn't really love her.

Love was the hardest emotion for me to grasp at that moment, and when I looked at my mom as she cried, I could only drop my gaze down to the floor. She walked into the sunroom, directly next to the kitchen, and closed the door. When I heard my dad coming from his study to the kitchen, I immediately jumped up and ran back down the hall.

I stood in the doorway of my room, my heart racing like I had run a marathon in record time, numb in all places yet surprisingly serene. My hands began to shake, then my legs. My heart felt like an object in my body and not a real part of me, something there just to take up space. Its pounding felt like someone was punching my chest as hard as he possibly could.

I held my arms up to the edges of the doorway and grasped them as I shook. I knew I would fall if I let go. My fragile, broken body was like a ragdoll's. It was a ragdoll that everyone was playing with. It was a ragdoll that the two boys had played with in that exercise room. It was a ragdoll that my parents would try to fix. It was a ragdoll that was permanently torn.

9 ∘ *doctor, doctor*

A few hours later, I overheard my parents in my dad's study discussing the phone call between my mom and uncle. I snuck out of my room to eavesdrop and heard my mom saying through tears, "This is worse than I thought. It's horrible. Those two boys doing those terrible things to her…and he had the audacity to blame this on her? I trusted him to take care of her and this happens! This is unforgivable."

"I know…it really is. I want to kill him." My dad spoke in an emotional voice that I did not recognize. I had never heard him cry, and he sniffled in a way that I knew his heart was broken too. I ran back to my room and locked the door. Sitting on the big black office chair next to my desk, I turned on my normal playlist with Maroon 5 and Snow Patrol, hoping to drown out any emotions I felt coming on. About an hour later, there was a soft knock on my door.

"Neesha, we're going to a clinic now, and you need to bring all the clothes you were wearing on New Year's Eve," my mom said.

Those simple words were all I received, and I didn't even bother questioning my mother at this point. I just did as she asked, unsure of what to expect. But there was something so disconcerting about the way she said it. It was a command, not a question or a request, and to me that made me feel how I felt in Houston. I went through my clothes and picked out the ones from that night. As the song changed, I looked out the window to notice that the sun had already set.

We drove to the Rape Crisis Center of Central New Mexico, but that never registered to me that night. I didn't realize I was going to have an examination. In my head, I had convinced myself that I wasn't raped.

I was sure I wasn't raped.

I wasn't raped.

I wasn't raped.

I wasn't raped.

I wasn't raped.

I wasn't raped.

Why were my parents taking me to this center when I wasn't raped? They knew I hated hospitals and anything resembling them. I had always dreaded the doctor's office. The smell of overly clean waiting rooms and alcohol swabs made me tremble. Even dentist offices bothered me.

After gathering my clothes and walking to the car, I had no idea why someone would need my favorite red volleyball shirt from summer camp, my black bra, my pink lace underwear, and my striped pajama pants. They had a white drawstring before New Year's Eve, but I noticed in the car that it was missing.

The drive consisted of me listening to my iPod and zoning out of any conversation that was taking place between my parents in the front seat. Thirty minutes later, my parents and I sat in an empty waiting room with light blue walls and giant glass windows. I could tell we were all anxious to hear my name. None of us wanted to be there.

I looked outside aimlessly. The dark sky was filled with stars, and the night was like any other New Mexico night—not the prettiest sight, just a desert with no light.

The cars that drove by were not very flashy. Old trucks and too many Hondas. The city lights outside didn't remind me at all of a real city. I didn't like this part of downtown Albuquerque very much, mainly because I thought it was trashy and unsafe. The part of town I lived in was beautiful. The Sandia Mountains were a work of art. I had the best view from my parents' upstairs porch. Sunsets turned the

Sandia Mountains pink, and the sky would fill with brilliant shades of orange, red, and pink until the sun disappeared. This really was the ideal place to grow up.

But I never appreciated it at the time.

In my head, I thought there was more out there in the world than the tiny town I called home. I thought about living in a place where no one knew me. An imaginary place to get lost in and a place to get found.

I was the anywhere-but-here girl. Especially now, in this rape crisis center.

Listening to my iPod in the waiting room was the only thing keeping me somewhat sane. The song "Must Get Out" by Maroon 5 came on as I turned up the volume to drown out my parents. The lonely song fit my mood. I pulled out my cell phone and texted Emma to distract myself even though I knew she was at jazz band practice. I wanted to tell her what was going on, but I didn't know what she would say. I had no desire to make a big deal out of this. But I missed being able to talk to her at any second of the day, so I mustered up a quick, *Hey, what's up?*

Neesha! How have you been? How was the rest of your day?

It was fine, you?

Mine was great, I'm actually at band right now, but let me give you a call right after!

I didn't respond, but I didn't really care. Worry overwhelmed my body, making me feel like I had a high fever in the middle of the desert. I could smell a mixture of old carpets and alcohol swabs, which made me want to gag. I wondered what would happen behind the two swinging gray doors that I couldn't stop staring at. I shook my head with dread. Patience never suited me well.

Another girl sat alone in the corner who seemed to be a few years older than me. She wore dark blue jeans, white tennis shoes, and a red hoodie from the University of New Mexico. I tried to fake a smile when she looked at me because I knew that's what my old self would have done. However, nothing was coming except a frown.

The nurse called my name, and I stood up as if my body were glass, ready to shatter.

Reluctantly, I gave her the plastic bag that contained my clothes. This all felt too foreign. I had no feeling or past experience to relate to. My clothes had always been mine but not on this night.

First the nurse had me pee in a cup to take a pregnancy test. I could not for the life of me figure out why she did this. I wasn't raped. I had convinced myself that none of these precautions were even remotely necessary. Because after all, I told myself, I wasn't raped.

I wasn't raped.

I wasn't raped.

I wasn't raped.

Taking that pregnancy test ensured that I was no longer a child. As I ripped the plastic wrapper, I said good riddance to being a normal fourteen-year-old. As I peed on the stick, I felt my childhood being banished. I knew there was no reason for this test, and it made me shiver with embarrassment to know those boys were to blame.

I blindly took a step into adulthood, a void of nothingness. I wasn't some careless girl who could be pregnant at fourteen. Why was I taking a pregnancy test? I could not figure it out. This made no sense.

Like that, I kissed away my innocence.

Walking out of the bathroom, I handed the nurse the pregnancy test and cup of urine.

"We usually would swab for evidence," she said as she took the test and cup, "but you've showered since this happened, right?"

"Yes. It's been like four days."

"As soon as you showered, the physical evidence was gone, but I still need to swab your mouth to collect DNA for DNA profiling," she explained.

I opened my mouth ever so slightly. Nothing like I had done a few nights before. She had to tell me to open wider. Only then did I realize how much my jaw still hurt from New Year's Eve.

She forced a long plastic swab into my mouth and rubbed it around—not a typical cotton swab but one that resembled a thermometer, a high-tech contraption that would be found on some crime television show. I quickly closed my mouth and moved my tongue around to moisten it.

She put the swab in a container of clear liquid. I saw a thin blue strip appear on it.

"You're not much of an eater, are you?" the nurse said. "The stick only turns blue if someone is seriously malnourished."

Get the hell out of my business, lady. "I'm fine."

She handed me a chocolate Balance Bar as she laughed. I tried to figure out what she was thinking as I glared at her.

"Eat this," she commanded. As if I would listen. Then she walked to the adjacent room to run tests with my urine sample and the swab.

Why did she tell me what to do? Why was everyone telling me what to do? Stop trying to control me.

I opened the bar and broke off a piece of chocolate chalk—then threw the whole bar in the trash. And suddenly, I felt strong—inconceivably strong, like I had more will power than anyone and I could refuse something that someone gave me. I hadn't been able to say no that night or to anything that my parents had made me do, like coming to this stupid place. I had no ability to refuse that either. Finally, I could say no to eating this bar.

The drive home with my parents managed to be worse than the drive from the airport. I wanted to kill them. Mortified and furious, I was completely ashamed of my body and myself. Why did they put me through this? I felt like a case study, completely dehumanized and detached.

I hated myself.

This hate was something new to me, some emotion I had never felt as a kid. This was not the hate that you feel when you fail a test and hate the teacher. This was not the hate you feel when the school bully knocks your ice cream cone out of your hand in the middle of summer or trips you on the way to recess causing you to skin your knee.

This was the hate you feel when you are absolutely disgusted with yourself, completely revolted. So sickened that you need to get out of your skin. As if maggots are crawling all over your body, all over your face, underneath your clothes, in your hair and in between your toes, but they will not go away as much as you try. You shake your arms and your legs in an attempt to get them off, but the more you shake the more they appear. An attempt to scream would only make things worse, and this level of discomfort would make anyone shut down.

Wishing I could shut my eyes and never wake up again was the only thought I had on this drive home. I wanted to close my eyes, my mind, and my body off to the rest of the world. Seeing a world of black would be better than the real world, and what was the point in trying to trek through the real world when you weren't who you thought you were? Because I was not the girl I used to be the moment I peed in that cup. When that moment took place, I was no longer fourteen anymore. I was no longer a kid.

I didn't want to feel, see, think, or hear anything or anyone anymore. I wanted to jump back a couple of years in my life and stay there forever. With my innocence intact and with a future.

10 ∘ *slamming doors*

After what felt like a decade in the car with my parents, we finally arrived home. I ran to my room and slammed the door as hard as I could, with the hope of making my parents jump when they heard the alarming noise. My blood pumped like I was on steroids; this only happened before big volleyball games or a final point against our rival team. This never happened in my life at home. I paced back and forth in my room, wanting to stay in there forever, needing to escape my parents. I wanted to shut those two out completely, after they made me go to the clinic and embarrass myself. When was I getting my clothes back anyway? They still had my favorite volleyball shirt.

The clock read 10:30 p.m., and I thought maybe I should at least try to lie down to catch my breath. After changing into my purple-and-white pajama pants and a black T-shirt, I crawled under the pink cotton sheets on my bed, thinking about the two boys who were responsible for this disaster. Why was I left to deal with it when they were able to live their lives as though nothing happened? Devastation overwhelmed my entire world, but they were home free.

"It's not fair," I said to myself.

There was a sudden knock on the door, and then the handle jiggled. "Honey?" my mom called.

Doesn't anyone respect that the door is closed? I want to be left alone.

"Yes?"

I slowly walked over to the door, unlocked it, and let my mom in.

"Are you okay?" she asked me.

Are you kidding me?

"Yes, I'm fine. I'm going to bed."

"Did you eat dinner? Do you want me to make you something?"

I want you to get away from me. "No, Mom. I'm going to bed!"

She looked at me for a few seconds as if she saw someone other than her daughter.

"Okay, well, I'm going to be calling my lawyer about what happened—and a detective, who will most likely want to interview you tomorrow over the phone. You'll be coming home from school early."

My breath started getting heavy as I began to bite my lower lip until it almost bled. I could not believe she was seriously turning this into a legal case. I was fine.

I was fine.

I was fine.

I was fine.

I was fine.

I would be fine if everyone would stop making this a big deal. Why was everyone blowing this so out of proportion? I went to bed that night hating myself even more than I had the night before. I refused to leave my room to eat any sort of dinner. It was too late, and what was the point?

I didn't care anymore.

The next morning, I lay in bed and looked at my body. I found nothing pretty about it. Not in a sense of being fat, because I knew I wasn't, but it did not feel like mine anymore. It felt like an object that no longer belonged to me. Knowing the ugly things it had been through on New Year's, I wished I still had the unharmed body from December 30.

I looked at my phone and saw a text from Brad asking me how I was doing. There was no point in responding, but I missed his compliments right now. I slowly shuffled to the bathroom to look at my face, but all I felt was shame. As I put my double-zero jeans on, my body hurt; the harsh denim stung and pricked at my skin. I had no motivation for school that day and didn't even bother doing my hair. Instead I put it in a messy ponytail, which made me look as if I hadn't showered. My ability to feel pretty was gone. I saw in my reflection a little fourteen-year-old girl—the girl I wished to be—but inside, I felt destroyed. My body was in a million pieces that would not fit back together. I would have given up anything at that moment just to be a little girl again.

11 ∘ *lose*
wednesday, january 4, 2006

That morning in my bathroom, I took a few deep breaths before getting on the white scale I kept underneath one of my two sinks. I weighed in at 87.5 pounds. Not terrible.

Walking into the kitchen, I glanced at a cup of coffee in my normal place on the counter. I grabbed it without adding any milk to it, just three Splendas. My mom looked over. "Do you want any milk with that?"

Can you not talk to me, please? "No. I'm fine."

"Okay, well, Dad will take you to school, but I'm going to be picking you up after your first two classes. A detective is going to call you about everything. I know you probably don't want to do any of this, but you're just going to have to. We need to get to the bottom of this."

I never missed school, but more than that, what was she talking about? I wanted nothing to do with this. My dad drove me to school as I chugged a bottle of water and sat there in silence. I slowly walked to my Algebra II and Geology classes with Brad, Jane, and Emma but didn't have much to say. I focused on drinking water during each class to try to clear out my system. Feeling as disgusting as I did, I thought a little cleanse would be a good way to feel clean.

"I haven't seen you in a while. You doing okay?" Brad asked me.

"Yeah, I'm fine. I have to leave after this class though."

"For what?"

Oh my god, stop with the questions. "Dentist appointment," I said as I rolled my eyes.

As I sat at my desk, I looked down at my legs and noticed that my jeans already looked looser. I smiled to myself for a second. Baggy jeans would become important for me during the month of January. If my jeans were falling off my body, then I was truly disappearing just like I wanted. I could rewind the clock to before these adult things happened to my childlike body. If I didn't have any curves or anything to resemble being a grown up, then I would be more like the kid I was before. I could be like everybody else again.

The bell rang, and I grabbed my backpack and books as quick as I could to avoid any sort of conversation with my friends.

"Bye, Neesha!" Emma tried to get in before I made it out the door, but I just mustered up a wave.

My walk to the office to sign out of school for the day was more of a slow saunter. Misery weighed my shoulders down, and I prayed that this would be the last of it. If I could just tell this stupid detective what happened, then it would have to be over, right?

Staying silent on the car ride home, plugged into my music, I ran into my room once my mom parked in the garage. I sat on my black chair with my knees to my chest. I felt safest that way—small enough to always fit in a ball, safe enough where no one could break me. But I ultimately knew I was broken now.

Staring at my white-carpeted floor, I couldn't even hold my legs up for more than a few seconds. I lost my balance and collapsed onto the floor, mentally and physically exhausted. Thoughts raced back and forth in my head. What was he going to ask me? Why did I have to relive this night once again? Last night's visit to the rape clinic had been humiliating enough, and I had no desire to talk about New Year's Eve ever again. I was finished with this and just wanted to move the hell on with my life.

But my parents thought differently.

I wanted them to respect that they were not getting the story out of me again. No one was. Why would I tell a stranger what I could not even formulate in my own mind?

I looked down at my body, angling my hips to see if my hipbones were more visible today. They weren't, and I felt useless. I still existed too much. I had only been fasting for a few days, but I wanted to be gone quicker, to disappear from this situation.

The phone finally rang. I jumped up like bread out of a toaster. I ran to the door and waited for my mom to walk down the hall with the phone. When she knocked a moment later, I opened the door and took the phone from her hand without saying a word. I then closed the door before she could say anything to me.

I can't believe this is happening. "Hello?"

"Hello, Neesha?" asked an older male voice. "This is Detective Reynolds, and I was wondering if I could ask you a couple of questions about what happened the night of New Year's Eve. Also, this conversation will be recorded to keep on file. Is that all right with you?"

"Sure."

"So, this happened on New Year's Eve?"

You just said that. "Yeah."

"Where were you?"

"My uncle's house. In Houston…"

"Can you tell me what happened that night?"

I don't want to talk about it. "Um…like what?"

"With you and those boys. Who was involved in what happened later that night?"

"What do you mean? It was two of my cousin Rob's friends. I left my other cousin's room after we went to bed."

"Then what happened?"

"I went to the living room," I said, my heart beginning to pound. "Then all of a sudden, we were in the exercise room. I was with my cousin's friends…"

"What were their names?"

Don't you already know all of this? "Mark and Will."

"So what happened with you three?"

I hesitated. "I thought my mom already told you."

"She did, Neesha, but I need to hear it from you. We're doing a lot of interviews, including everyone that was there that night, but I need to hear your side of the story," he told me.

"Um…I don't know." My heart began to pound even faster, and my stomach turned. A bitter taste in my mouth formed. "I mean, it was dark, and like I was in the room, and I just couldn't really move. I tried to leave, but I just couldn't."

"What time was it?"

"I don't know. I think it was like two in the morning."

"Did they make you do things that you didn't want to do?"

But I just couldn't bring myself to say anything out loud again. It hurt too much to say those words. After telling Jane once, I refused to listen to someone who wanted me to tell the story again. "Um…"

He continued with his obnoxious questioning, then he told me that the only way to press charges against the two boys for sexual abuse or possibly rape was for me to testify against them in court. There was no physical proof for them to investigate besides my clothes from that night, which didn't have any evidence.

I fell completely silent during this part of the phone conversation. I couldn't do it. I had no desire to fight against the two boys.

I had already given up.

He proceeded to tell me about the legal procedure that would have to be followed in order to make it a case. As I listened, my body quivered, just like it did on New Year's Eve. I didn't know what was happening. My heart and mind raced like I was on drugs. My body temperature rose, and sweat started dripping down my forehead. Even as an athlete, I rarely sweat. I touched my face—warm and damp— and couldn't believe I was drenched in sweat while having a phone conversation. On edge and irritated, I suddenly felt acid coming up my throat.

"Look," I said when the detective's questioning finally stopped,

"I'm, like, fourteen. I just can't talk about it, and I don't want to. I mean, we were in an exercise room, and everything happened really fast. It was dark and super overwhelming, and I mean, I don't even know. I don't remember."

"Can you tell me who specifically was in the house that night?"

I stood up and started pacing around my room, staring at the white carpet.

Please stop asking me questions. "Rob and Anita, Will and Mark, my aunt and uncle once they got home." I rubbed my damp forehead. "There were a couple of Anita's friends that I don't really know—Kate and Lisa. I met them that night."

"Where was everyone else while you, Will, and Mark were in the exercise room?"

"Their bedrooms, I guess. Anita's friends were in her room. They were all sleeping, I'm assuming."

I couldn't figure out how this was even relevant at the time. If they were going to make a case out of it, why would they need to know who was sleeping that night? They were clearly not in the exercise room with the three of us, so how did they even factor in? I was beginning to get more and more aggravated with this brainless detective. I thought he should do his job better and ask questions that actually pertained to everything that happened and ask them quickly. He was not going to get answers to those questions, not from me, but he should have considered getting to the point. Maybe if he had asked clear questions and not such invasive ones, I would have answered them.

Or maybe not.

Once the detective finally gave up, I muttered a quick goodbye and took the phone back to the kitchen, where my mom sat reading the newspaper. For a split second in the hall, my mind flashed back to Houston but not the incident. It flashed back to Anita and Rob and the fact that they didn't even try to comfort me. They never took my side. Maybe Rob felt like he couldn't talk to me, but that was no excuse. Anita and I had been so close—why hadn't she called me since I left? I snapped back to reality and saw my mother in the kitchen. She never even asked me if I wanted this legal case.

"How'd it go?"

"Fine," I mumbled, wanting to push her down a hill.

"Tell me what he asked. Is everything okay? Don't be upset. You really need to just trust him and do what he asks. He's only trying to help you."

Everyone needs to *stop* trying to help me. "Yeah."

"I made you a sandwich: turkey and cheese. You can eat it in your room. I know you're not really in the talking mood, but I promise, we're all trying to help fix this for you."

"Thanks," I slurred. I shuffled back to my room before she could ask for more details and slammed the door.

I began pacing again after I set the glass plate on my desk. Trying to take a bite of what used to be one of my favorite lunch foods, I put it back down and chewed the bite almost twenty times before swallowing it. I tried to contemplate why I had just been forced to retell my story even in bits and pieces to the detective. Then I wondered how my mom had the nerve to passively ask me how it went. My legs felt like they were burning, but it was just my muscles tensing as I walked back and forth across my room as fast as I could.

My heart pounded, and my thoughts shifted back to New Year's Eve. I crossed my hands against my forehead, stared down at the floor, and then began to let out a few sighs that soon turned into quiet tears. Flashbacks of the boys' faces in the dark exercise room played in my mind. I saw them, and I heard their aggressive voices. I hated that I thought Will had the nicest eyes before any of this happened. He had the longest eyelashes I had ever seen. I thought he was perfect, but now I despised myself for having those thoughts that night. I loathed myself for being so stupid. How completely pathetic was I for letting this happen? What the hell was wrong with me?

I must have brought that night on myself, I thought in disgust, since I thought he was attractive. This was my fault, and I was making not only myself miserable but everyone else.

Only a lost soul has these thoughts, I supposed. Not the mature young adult I wanted to be. I thought that I was being an adult on New Year's Eve, hanging out in the living room with my cousins and Rob's older friends. I thought it was a night of maturity, to be laughing and talking with two seventeen-year-old boys, but it wasn't. What did I know about being an adult?

I finally sat down and tried to come up with reasons for the terrible turn that night had taken, but I could not think of any. I replayed the night in my mind over and over. I couldn't stop beating myself up. I would think one moment, Why did I do this? This is completely my fault. Then anger would grip me and I thought, No, it was completely Will's fault.

Every other second, I would remember how forced everything was. Unable to sort through my emotions and thoughts, I was left with one question: *Why me?*

I could not figure out why I had to be the one sitting on the floor, dealing with the aftermath. What did I do that was so terrible for this to happen to me? Helpless and lost, I did not want to play the victim, but it began to tear me up inside. *Why did they do this to me?*

Fourteen with no answers. I needed someone to tell me why this happened to me. I did not need to hear that the two boys were "stupid" or "bad people" or anything else that would excuse them. Beneath everything I felt, I wanted to know why they did this to *me*.

12 ∘ *not to need*
thursday - sunday, january 5-8, 2006

The loss of my self-respect never struck me then, but the previous week had thrown it away. Maybe it was the rape clinic that made me think I wasn't a good girl anymore, maybe it was Mark and Will who made me feel like a toy, or maybe it was because I no longer felt like the daughter I used to be for letting this entire situation happen. But whatever it was, it never occurred to me that I lost more than my innocence on New Year's. I lost my dignity, and for that, there was no telling what I would do next. I just knew I hated myself.

Uncertainty began to overcome me in odd ways over the next few days. I started having a hard time trusting boys or talking to them. Even being in the presence of males brought me back to that night and the way I felt in the exercise room. Panic and trauma were a result of Will thinking I was pretty, and I couldn't shake that feeling of what could happen if someone else saw me that way.

I was afraid to leave the house, afraid to be alone, afraid to be with people.

I didn't think fear could strike a fourteen-year-old as hard as it struck me. I was not out for revenge against the boys or my family in Houston, but I was hoping everything would just go away. I wanted to rewind time to be a normal girl again, but my mind thought differently.

It never stopped reminding me that I needed to be punished for letting this happen.

The night before I avoided dinner by taking my plate of salmon, potatoes, carrots, and bread to my room, hoping I wouldn't have to sit with my parents at the dinner table.

"Mom, I'm really not feeling well. Can I just go eat in my room?"

"I would appreciate it if you would eat with us," my mom responded.

"Just let her go, hon. Yeah, you can eat in your room if you want," my dad interjected.

Walking slowly as I held my plate, my black sweatpants dragged on the floor, but I didn't care to roll them up. I nibbled at the carrots and took five bites of salmon before taking the rest to the bathroom to flush down the toilet. With only a little bit of bread on my plate, I shuffled slowly back to the kitchen to hear my mom speaking.

"I want to see those boys in jail. There better be terror in their eyes when the detectives show up."

"I know, me too. I want to go over there and—" my dad began to say.

As I walked in, they turned back to the nightly news on TV. I faked a smile and set my plate in the sink. My parents were eager to send those boys to jail, but I just wanted to be able to hang out with Jane, Emma, and the volleyball team again. I had always fit in, been part of the crowd, one of the girls, and all of a sudden I did not feel like I was one of them anymore. Wishing I could be carefree again, I knew I wasn't an adult but, rather, I felt tainted and dirty. My friends did not know this side of fear or pain or the desire to feel empty all the time. It was the side that kept me up at night with cold tears in my eyes. I knew when I closed them only nightmares would appear. Nightmares that were my reality. The image of testifying against Will in court became all too vivid, and I wanted to forget about him completely.

What would I wear to court? How could I hide my body in such a way that it wouldn't be able to be violated by him? If I had to see those two boys again, how would I know they wouldn't come near me again? After all, Mark made me hug him goodbye the day after he did those terrible things.

Questions and more questions sent me into a panic. My body was constantly moving, shaking, or fidgeting. If it stood still, my mind took over. I would start to overheat, and enough sweat would form to wet my bangs.

I wanted to deaden everything inside me.

Even though it had only been a couple of days, I had a constant stomachache, the anxious kind that makes it grumble even though you aren't hungry. Distracting myself and keeping busy was harder than anticipated, but I needed to numb my feelings instead of getting emotional and showing weakness. I didn't want to accept what happened.

The sense of worthlessness overflowed inside me as if I was just taking up space. Within days, my self-value was gone—and it was not coming back anytime soon.

I had the determination of a champion bodybuilder. Only he would lift his way to the top, and I would starve myself to the bottom. I wanted to be far away, in my own world, and starvation felt like it could be its own world to me. Heading in blindly, I imagined starvation would be a world where I could be alone without a haunting memory.

Trying to be by myself more than normal, I avoided the kitchen, where I was more likely to see my parents. After school I would say the bare minimum to my mom as she made me green tea, then I would take it to the oversized blue couch in the living room and watch TV.

I knew my parents were worried. I could see it in their faces, but there was no way I would open up when they were pushing this legal case on me. They did not understand that I couldn't handle it. I just couldn't. What hurt the most was that they never asked me if I would be okay with this or if I even wanted it. They never asked me if I wanted to face the boys in court or if I would be willing to. And the truth is, I never would be.

Maybe they thought it was part of dealing with what happened, a phase they needed to let me work through, but my isolation was clearly hurting them. I felt guilty that they had to watch helplessly as their only daughter suffered, but I simply could not act like everything was okay. I was no longer the person I used to be, and having them push this on me made me resent them because I was trying to forget and move on. I was so ashamed of myself that I didn't want them to even look at me. I couldn't accept their hugs. If they managed to sneak one in, it was always forced. Before New Year's I would hug them twice a day at least.

During dinners, I would try to eat a little bit of the food that my mom prepared, but I always found a way to eat in my room. "Mom, I need to talk to Jane about a homework assignment, so can I just eat in my room?"

"Neesha," my mom would ask every evening that week, "why won't you just sit with us?"

"I really just want to be alone, and I really need to talk to Jane."

"Didn't you just see her at school?"

"Yeah, I have homework that I'm trying to figure out."

"This is getting ridiculous."

You are the one being ridiculous. "It's just homework. Everything is fine."

"No, Neesha. Why can't you do it after dinner?"

"Because she has things to do. Let me just go make this phone call. Please!"

"You need to be a part of the family!"

You need to stop with the legal case and leave me alone. "I am."

"No, you need to be here at the table for dinner. Why don't you want to sit with us anymore?"

"Mom, I'm eating dinner. I'm just not eating it here at the table. Why does it even matter?" I would snap, and she would almost cry. I no longer felt up to family dinners even though I would always eat with my parents before. Having the power to say no to food gave me a sense of strength and a coping mechanism. I had the chance to change the way my life was going, and for the first time since New Year's, I could control my own fate.

I quickly absorbed myself in my loneliness. I didn't really have any phone calls to make, and my homework was not getting done, which was not like my perfectionist self. I thought if I could find the strength to deal with that night on my own, then I would be invincible, and this was the only way I knew how. To me, there was no other option. If I managed to go through my entire day by myself, then I would somehow be back in the driver's seat of my life.

13 ∘ *losing your way*
january, 2006

"Neesha, are you okay?" Jane whispered while the teacher worked out a problem on the board. "You look really sick. You should eat something. Do you want my sandwich?"

"No, I'm fine," I said with my head on the desk, facing away from her. With my crossed arms I held my stomach, trying to hide the pain I felt. "I just didn't sleep well last night, that's all."

"I have an orange, if that's better. Really, just take it. I'll leave it in your backpack for later if you don't want it now."

"No, it's really fine. I just need to drink some water."

"Neesha, I'm worried about you. So are Brad and Emma. Are you sure you're okay?"

"Yeah, I'm totally fine. I promise." I lifted my head to turn and give her a fake smile.

Could she see the bags under my eyes or tell that I was blatantly lying? Jane had been one of my best friends for years, and I knew she would be okay with me complaining a little—after all, she knew what happened that night. She never brought it up after my mom talked to her, thankfully. We acted like nothing ever happened. For the next few days, I would have the orange from Jane in my stomach, and that was it.

In mid-January on a Tuesday, with no energy left after school, I hoped I could squeeze in a run to burn more calories, but I decided to take a nap to take my mind off food or feelings, to give myself a break. I poked my head into the kitchen and forced a smile at my mom. "I'm just going to head to my room—I have a lot of homework, and I'm really tired, so I probably won't be eating until later. I might take a nap."

"Okay, but you should really have a snack. How was school?" she asked as she looked up from reading the newspaper. My mom drank a cup of English breakfast tea every afternoon and asked about my day ever since I could remember.

"Mom, I ate the sandwich you made me, and I'm still full. Brad and I had a bunch of snacks too, but I'm really tired, so I'm going to head to bed."

"Just come catch up for a second first."

Snow fell outside on that January afternoon, but my kitchen had enough heat in it to melt every flake. Grateful for the warmth, I still had on my pink Ugg boots, my double-zero dark blue jeans, and my puffy white jacket. My clasped hands were freezing, but the discomfort took my mind off anything serious.

I took a seat in the kitchen against my will, thinking I should put in a little effort. "It was good. I'm just so tired, though." My head was pounding, the kitchen was spinning, and the act of talking was becoming tougher and tougher. "I slept terribly last night."

My mom reached out to give me a hug. "Are you okay? You don't look good at all. Go get some rest, honey."

"Okay. I don't know, maybe I'm getting a cold?" I sounded like a robot, and I felt like one as I stumbled down the hall to my room.

Changing into my black sweatpants with two white stripes down each side, the drawstring felt looser than usual as I looked at my tiny stomach. I tightened it. My imperfections were a constant reminder that I hadn't forgiven myself and that the pain still existed.

I walked over to my full-length mirror with pink, green, purple, and white flowers painted on the edges and stared at my body. I took off my jacket and pulled up my blue T-shirt. I could barely see my hipbones, and for the first time my stomach looked way too big.

I turned sideways and sucked in my stomach as much as I could. Seeing it shrink made me appreciate the hunger pains—validation of what I was doing. I knew it was working, but I still blamed myself for everything that happened in Houston.

I let out a brief whimper and threw my hands to my hips, thinking they were massive as I hit them as hard as I could. The pain made me cry out. In frustration, I turned off the lights and jumped into my bed. I pulled the comforter over my face and continued to cry. Attempting to sleep, I merely sniffled for an hour. I wished the silence of being alone made me relax, but I realized I hadn't had a moment of relaxation since before New Year's. My heart constantly beat at the pace of a clock on double-time no matter what I did. Whether it was sitting in the car on my way to school in the morning or simply trying to fall asleep, I constantly tried to escape, but I only ran into my own thoughts.

Lying in my bed, staring at the ceiling, hoping I could make it all vanish, I wanted everything to go back to how it used to be. Wishing I could just call Emma or Brad to make my day happier, I still couldn't bear telling them the story. Curling into a ball, I kept feeling my face getting damper and damper. I only ever cried alone, but now I was always alone.

After my nap, I put on my volleyball state championship pink hooded sweatshirt. I found more comfort in my hunger after lying in my bed for an hour, able to appreciate it when the stomach pain ceased. Now dark outside, it was about 5:30 p.m.

I opened my door and decided to face my parents while they ate dinner. I heard the news on television as I walked into the kitchen, hoping that they wouldn't notice me.

"I'm getting a little concerned about her. She's not eating with us and looks exhausted. I've never seen her look like this before," my mom said.

"I mean, she needs to start eating dinner with us, bottom line. She spends no time with us anymore and is silent on our car rides. She just listens to that damn iPod," my dad responded.

I waited until I heard them go silent when the news came back on. My parents turned to face me as I entered the room. I tried not to acknowledge them at all. I picked up a glass and grabbed a can of Diet Coke out of the refrigerator.

"Aren't you going to eat dinner, Neesha?" my mom asked.

I fake-smiled at her as I headed toward the hall. "I'll eat later. Too much homework."

"But I made your favorite pasta, and I have chocolate chip cookies for dessert."

One of my favorite meals. "Mom, I am just not in the mood. Do you really want me to fail my classes? I need to go work on my homework."

"Neesha, you can't talk to me like that! What's gotten into you?"

"I just don't want to eat dinner right now!"

Snotty and cold, I thought if we argued, I could avoid eating dinner. I took the water back to my room and opened up my laptop on my bed to the website LiveJournal, an online blog where people chronicle their lives. But this time I found blogs on the site that contained dieting tips. I curled up under my covers without even a thought about my homework. I knew it wasn't going to get done. How could I focus on homework? All my energy was spent on distracting myself from that night.

With a sigh I tossed my books and notepads to the floor and closed the tab of the blog. It only frustrated me that I couldn't have the self-control like everyone on the website. Girls had posted their statistics: height, weight, and BMI. I didn't know mine off the top of my head, but I knew I would never weigh myself at night. I knew I was heavier then. Flustered at all the numbers, I turned up the music on my blue laptop. Listening to music was all I did these days.

For me, it was always music.

The words made it easier to cope and gave me something to relate to, such as "Please take me away from here"—I could understand a line like that. Those little details in songs kept me going but also kept me sad. Music made the drive to school bearable.

I began searching the Internet constantly, mainly looking up food or researching blogs to motivate me to stay strong. Just a bit of a distraction at first, but I quickly became obsessed, and my reality of New Year's started to fade.

14 ∘ *best friends*

end of january, beginning of february, 2006

I began lying to Emma, Jane, and Brad. I told them that I had eaten a big breakfast in the morning with my parents and my stomach hurt from it. The three of us had always managed to get the same math and science classes together even though Brad and I were never as smart as Jane and Emma, but we always made a joke out of it. I felt guilty lying to them, but I didn't think I had a choice. After class on a Wednesday, Brad tracked me down despite my subtle exit.

"I have to go to the library. I wish I could talk, but I just have a lot of work to do."

"Neesha, why are you avoiding me? You don't have work to do. I'm in all your classes. This is such crap. What did I do?"

"You didn't do anything. I just really don't want to talk right now. I'm sorry."

Brad stormed off, confused as hell. But I no longer cared the way I would have a month before. Emma tried asking me if I would be eating with her on Thursday, but I said I had a meeting with a teacher. Lie.

They didn't ask me again on Friday.

Sitting in back of the classroom on Friday, I grew unnervingly cold. But it wasn't just goose bumps; I was cold from the bones. I tried on my pink tank top that morning, but it wasn't getting any looser—or at least I thought it wasn't. I had not eaten a single thing except the bare minimum at dinners. I just drowned myself in green tea, coffee, Diet Coke, and water. I dreaded knowing my weight. Rather than paying attention to what my teacher was telling our class, I told myself that I would weigh myself on Sunday morning to ensure that I was at my lowest. I opened my second bottle of water since lunch and tried to flush out my body, petrified of the scale already.

Starvation felt easy. So did denial.

Friday night, I was actually able to nap after school since I slept terribly all week. The nights that week had been filled with flashbacks of New Year's. Closing my eyes felt better than looking at the four walls surrounding me; in the dark my room began to feel like the exercise room. I began keeping my door open when I went to bed, afraid of confinement. I didn't know how to get the images out of my mind. I wished that it had been a dream, a nightmare rather. I just wished that the memory could go away.

The darkness felt quieter than usual, but for some reason, the silence kept me awake. Whether it was a creak in the roof or the desert wind outside, the slightest noise shot me into the air. Occasionally the sounds of New Mexico would fill my room—a coyote howling or the snow that turned into rain on my window—they became lucid. No matter what noises were there, I was never complacent enough to rest. The darkness killed any moment I might have felt at ease, and I found myself lost in the shadows. If I woke up to walk to the bathroom across the hall, there was no telling if I would walk into a wall as I felt my way there. Simply a maze in my own house, it no longer felt like the home it used to be.

When I woke up Saturday morning at 8:15 a.m. sharp, I was looking forward to having nothing to do all day. It would be easier for me not to eat if I didn't have to exert myself. I ran over to the mirror and lifted up my sweatshirt to do my daily check. My hipbones were more visible. Slight progress. Feeling a little satisfied, I went to the kitchen and poured myself a cup of coffee. My stomach turned over and let out a roar, which to me was a sweet noise of satisfaction and achievement. Almost light-headed, I was in a state of bliss I had never experienced after doing something like this.

I shuffled into the living room and watched the Food Network for the next four hours. It began to be a challenge to watch those shows and not eat. It made my body feel somewhat satisfied to see the delicious meals being prepared and consumed. I was obsessed with food and missed how before any of this I never gave two thoughts to what I was eating. Rachael Ray's *30-Minute Meals* was on, and I watched two episodes. Then it was Sandra Lee's *Semi-Homemade Cooking*. I loved these shows. They were the perfect escape from reality. Since there was nothing in my stomach, they nourished the part of my mind that was dying for nutrition.

Around 1:00 p.m., I dragged myself off the couch and went for a run even though my dad and I argued about it. I stormed out anyway and began running. Well, it was more of a slow jog. My body would not go faster than that, and even at my slow pace, my lungs were stinging. I walked for a mile up and down the park road by my house. It had a clear view of the horizon to the west and the Sandia Mountains to the east. I stopped at the bottom of my road to catch my breath, but my nostrils burned as if someone had shoved a Q-tip up them hard enough for it to break in half. I trembled in the freezing cold; my body shook, and my bones felt brittle. Probably about thirty degrees outside, the chill stiffened my joints.

Snow began to fall, hitting me softly in the face. Perfect, I thought as I turned to walk home. I tried to motivate myself to run the rest of the way, but my legs were beyond numb at this point. I had my leggings on under my black sweatpants, along with a white T-shirt, pink sweatshirt, black hat, and my beloved puffy white coat. I held my iPod in my red gloves.

I just needed earmuffs. How could I have been so stupid to not think to bring earmuffs? Rage began to build inside my chest. I was not sure how to deal with this unexpected anger with myself over something so trivial, but I was furious. The littlest things pissed me off lately. I never used to be so short-tempered, but now everything sent me overboard.

Walking in a huff, I made it to my house and brushed the snow off my tennis shoes. I closed the porch door behind me and stormed through the halls.

"Neesha, I don't think you should be outside. It's freezing!"

"I'm fine. It's not that bad out there."

"What do you want to eat? I'll make you whatever you want for dinner tonight," my mom called out as I passed the kitchen.

"Mom, I'll make something later," I growled.

As I mumbled ridiculous comments about the snow and earmuffs under my breath, I threw down my gloves and took off my socks and shoes. Incredibly apprehensive over nothing, I jumped into my bed and curled up in a ball under my two comforters. I tried to nap for a few hours but simply dozed in and out of sleep.

When I woke up at 5:00 p.m., I watched television again. This time it was *Iron Chef America*. My parents ate their dinner in the kitchen while I ate the sandwich my mother made for me in the living room. After my show, I snuck back to my room. I tried to go to bed at 9:30 p.m. every night, whether I slept or not.

The week finally ended, and it was time to weigh myself Sunday morning. I walked into my bathroom at 8:30 a.m. and used the toilet to make sure I was completely rid of anything left in my body. I stared at myself in the two mirrors and stood on my bathtub to get a good look at my legs. My thighs did not even touch, but I was convinced that they still existed too much. I pulled out my scale and set it on the white tile. Still wearing my black sweatpants and pink tank top, I stepped on the scale with my heart racing and my empty stomach cramping.

I looked down to read 85.5 pounds. Four and a half pounds so far.

Smiling to myself, I felt a tiny victory, but I did not feel whole. It was a quick moment of achievement, but I knew I hadn't won. I had not forgiven myself for what happened with the two boys.

The end of January turned into a routine of avoiding everyone. I would go to school and doze off. I wouldn't really talk to anyone except for Jane, Brad, and Emma while sitting in the back of every class.

None of us were mature enough to really understand the extent of the damage of that night, but I could not keep it in any longer. I finally broke down one day after school with Brad, but luckily Jane was with us.

The three of us went to the library after school, but I couldn't sit still. Staring at my legs in the wooden chair, I tried to remember our afternoons the year before—constant laughing and even occasional food fights, and Brad and I would raid the vending machines every day after school. I would get sour cream and onion potato chips and M&Ms, and he'd get peanut butter cups and pretzels. I would usually hog the M&Ms, but Brad always gave me one of the two peanut butter cups. He was always better at sharing, but this time there was no candy.

Jane looked at me. "Neesha, are you okay?"

"Umm, no. I just have to get this out."

"What's going on?" Brad asked me with a look of sympathy.

"Look, I need to talk to you about something that I've been avoiding because it's just really bad and I don't even know how to tell you. Jane knows...and...um...it was over New Year's Eve in Houston. Basically I was with my cousin's friends and..." I looked at Jane with tears in my eyes, but I could not say the words.

"Neesha, don't worry. I can tell him for you. I know it's really hard for you."

"I just can't. Have Jane tell you, Brad. I can't even say this. I have to go. I'm sorry." I ran out of the library.

I couldn't think about telling my only guy friend whom I loved so much. I just couldn't say any of those disgusting words.

Even though Jane told Brad, I knew I had to be the one to tell Emma. It had been a couple days since Brad found out, and he sent me a very sweet text message telling me how sorry he felt. When I finally worked up the courage to spend my free period with Emma again, I bit my lip in fear.

Rain poured outside as we sat in the cafeteria. I watched Emma eat her breakfast burrito without thinking of calories or fat. One of my favorite foods. For a moment, I was so jealous. She was the smallest person I'd ever seen. Five feet tall and 85 pounds without even trying, Emma was everything I wanted to be. A normal, beautiful fourteen-year-old girl. I admired her innocence and that she still remained pure in the eyes of boys. She didn't have the fear I had every time I would be in the same room as boys. In fact, she didn't have any fear. She wasn't afraid of the dark, or a noise in the distance, or who was walking behind her.

Her childhood was still intact. She didn't know the bottomless feeling in the pit of my stomach every time I heard the phone ring. Was it going to be the detective wanting to talk to me about Houston? She could still have a crush on a boy and imagine their New Year's kiss. She would wear a sparkly dress, and he would wear a button-down shirt. Emma could imagine her fairy tale and actually have it. She could find her Prince Charming and be Cinderella without having the constant visual of an exercise room in her mind.

She had everything to look forward to: her first kiss and the first time a boy touched her and changed her entire life for the better. Emma had the textbook definition of love to look forward to, and I didn't anymore. I no longer knew what that meant to me.

As I watched the rain outside, the smell of the burrito made my mouth water, and I quickly snapped back to the elephant in the room. Emma had a surprising amount of maturity and respected my boundaries. She knew I was keeping her at arm's length, but she was the one person in my life I told everything to.

Sitting at one of the long gray tables in the cafeteria, I fiddled with a napkin.

"So, how's everything going?" I asked.

"It's good. Where have you been hiding lately?" She put her burrito down. "Why have you been missing so much school, Neesha? What's been going on?"

"Well, you know how I went to Houston to visit my cousins?"

"Yeah, what happened?"

"Just, like, some stuff. I don't know. It really wasn't good."

"Are you okay?"

"I mean, honestly, no."

"It's kind of confusing, and I don't even really know." I took a deep breath as my heart began to pound. "But the reason I've been missing school is because basically I had to go to this doctor's office the other week, and just a bunch of other stuff."

Emma stared at me for a few seconds as she squinted her eyes. She knew something was up—how could she not? "What do you mean? What happened?"

"I mean two of my cousin's friends and I were in this room, and..." I bit my lip as I tried to breathe. "Things moved pretty fast, and it's all sort of a blur. I didn't want to do anything but..." Again I trailed off.

Emma reached across the table to take my hand. "Are you okay?"

"Mark was in the room. Mark and this other guy," I whispered. "And they were both doing things." Tears burned my eyes. "We didn't have sex, but—well—you know. They made me..."

"Oh my god," Emma said softly, eyes wide. She squeezed my hand. "I'm so sorry."

"Basically Mark fingered me and like—"

"Oh my god, what! He's your cousin's best friend!"

"I know, I know."

"What happened with the other guy, who was it?"

"Mark's friend, this guy Will. I met him over Thanksgiving. I thought he was cute and like, I don't know. I didn't want any of this to happen."

"What happened with Will?"

I took a deep breath as I began shaking. "He made me give him..."

And just like that, I didn't even have to finish the sentence.

Putting her hand over her mouth in shock, she had a look on her face that I had never seen before. It was a look of desperation for her best friend. A look of concern. Emma was hurting for me, but I didn't want that for her.

I looked away, trying not to let a teardrop fall.

I desperately wanted a hug and to cry the tears that meant something with my best friend, but I couldn't. I couldn't even hug her or handle the closest person touching me because it hurt too much. If I hugged her, I knew I would break down, and I didn't want her to see me be weak. I pulled my hand out of hers.

From that moment on, I didn't want to burden her with something I was not even mature enough to understand. I would see her every single day and never mention a word about how I was feeling. She never pressed me about that night or criticized my attitude or behavior. She was just there for me, quietly, steadily, like always.

Having a best friend who represented everything I wanted to be made it harder for me—her small frame, childlike attitude, all her innocence. It was difficult to see Emma's perfection and then look in the mirror at myself. We used to be so similar, and now everything had changed. I had changed.

Emma was the type of friend who could always cheer me up. Just seeing her face reminded me that eventually everything would be all right. She had an ability to always be okay and gave me hope I could too. If I hadn't had a best friend like her, I don't think the miserable nights I spent in my room would have been tolerable. Just the texts she sent in the middle of the night were enough to give me the strength to fake a smile—*I love you* or *I hope you're okay*. The moments I would see her at school were the ones when I could breathe a little easier. I knew I wasn't completely alone because of her.

There was something so significant about our friendship, even at the age of fourteen. She was the only person that really understood me by just a look.

One Tuesday in the beginning of February, we sat in the library reading magazines during our free period. As always, I wore my double-zero jeans and pink Uggs. The pink tank top I bought in Texas was underneath my white jacket, now fitting loosely. I weighed in at 83.5 pounds that morning, and I remember thinking about that number as I sat next to Emma.

We laughed and joked about the magazines we were reading, but the thing that really had my attention was that my legs were smaller than hers. For the first time ever, I registered that I was skinnier than the best friend I wanted to be like. Maybe if I was her size I could be a normal kid again, just like Emma.

For the first time, not eating felt like it paid off. I was little, just like a kid. I was able to turn back the clock, and for a moment I felt like nothing had happened on New Year's, like maybe I could reverse the damage that was done.

15 ∘ *wearing out*
february, 2006

I was dealing with the constant reminder of New Year's even though I was desperately trying to forget. My life was a constant question: Why did this happen to me?

I couldn't figure out the answer. Was there an answer?

Trying to move on with my life, I thought blocking out the assault with a new obsession could solve the problem. I thought if I could push that night far enough away, I could forget about it.

February continued, and I thought it was a blessing that the month from hell was gone. I felt like I was able to make it through the days, but the mornings were the hardest part because I would wake up and run to the mirror to look at my body. My head was full of questions all night, and in the morning after maybe three or four hours of sleep I would stare at my hips from every angle.

Every morning was the same. After putting on my white jacket and jeans, I walked out to my kitchen and sat down, already exhausted. I made useless conversation with my mom while she made my coffee, a burrito, and my lunch. I thanked her, carried everything to the car, and waited for my dad until it was time to go. Down to a strict routine. I plugged myself into my iPod and sipped my coffee on the way to school.

February turned into a cold, bitter month, but I still wondered why my cousins never reached out to me. As the winter seemed to never end and snow continued to fall, I thought about one of my favorite holidays: Christmas. On Christmas Eve, my mom and I would always light luminarias—a New Mexican tradition—small lanterns made of paper bags with a candle inside. Then my dad would read *T'was the Night Before Christmas* before we would all go to sleep. Even though I always spent Christmas in Albuquerque, there was something so special about the gifts I received from my family in Houston.

Anita and I were always given something that matched, like an outfit or a necklace. One year it was a pink jewelry box with a dancing ballerina that popped up and spun when you opened the box. Another year they gave me a pink Juicy Couture sweat suit that my parents wouldn't let me buy because they thought it was frivolous and a waste of money. Maybe it was. My parents had always been very reasonable about what they bought for me, but they gave me more than I could ever need. However, my aunt and uncle saw life differently. They dropped excessive money on designer clothes, which at the time very much excited me.

Every Christmas morning I would open their gifts first, but I could tell my parents were slightly uncomfortable to see me excited over something so unnecessary. Even when we were younger, Anita and I both had enormous collections of Beanie Babies, and my aunt sent me the three I couldn't find anywhere in Albuquerque. They had outbid everyone else on Ebay and spent hundreds of dollars on toys I probably would have no interest in the following year. Maybe it was because I complained too much to my cousins about the things I wanted that they already had, but I don't think I was ever ungrateful for what I did have. I don't think my aunt and uncle were doing anything other than trying to make their favorite niece happy, but they still knew my parents raised me differently. Everything in Houston had much more emphasis on materialism and extravagance whereas in Albuquerque, life was plentiful but not excessive. I never appreciated that until now. I never wanted to set foot in Houston again.

As February went on, I tried to keep up my runs after school, but I barely had the energy. If I couldn't finish the run or had to start walking, I would become enraged with myself.

During my runs that month, I started to feel a stinging pain in my knees from the weather—not quite like they were going to break but more of a bitter pain, like when a child stands on her toes, breaks a toenail, and rips it off. With my knees aching, I would head to bed, trying to avoid any conversation with anyone.

On Tuesday, February 14, Valentine's Day, I woke up for school and did my morning routine like every other day. I began my day in the bathroom, but I didn't weigh myself that morning. I decided to give myself a slight break. I had no desire to think about boys, and I was not about to go to any Valentine's parties that night. The thought of seeing boys and girls together maturing into that adult stage of affection made my stomach flip. Wishing I could spend it with Brad, my favorite boy in the world, I just couldn't find it in me to enjoy this day with my friends. No longer possessing my childhood or innocence, the only boys that were on my mind were still Will and Mark.

I wanted my childhood back, the days in elementary school when everyone gave the Barbie Valentine's cards with a chocolate kiss in them. I missed elementary school. It was so simple.

Walking down the hall from my room, I noticed snow was still falling outside. I remembered the year before, when I spent Valentine's Day with Brad, Emma, and Jane. It made me realize that things were not the same at all. Even Anita had sent me a gift last year, but now that friendship was gone. That whole part of my family was gone. I sat down in the kitchen and saw that my mom had given me a heart-shaped box full of chocolate.

"Happy Valentine's Day, babe!" she exclaimed as she came over and tried to hug me.

"Thanks—you too," I muttered as I stared at the chocolate that sat on my blue placemat. Charlie Brown's and Snoopy's faces smiled on the front of the box, along with the other happy, innocent characters.

But it just reminded me that I had no warm, fuzzy feelings. They no longer filled me the way they used to as I looked at the box. I would never eat the chocolate that was in there, and the whole concept bothered me. I had no desire to even smile that morning.

16 ∘ *move in circles (detective's second call)*

february - march, 2006

Weeks had passed, and I was still stunned that my cousins had not taken my side. I couldn't understand why I had not heard from them, and the weight of the blame intensified my tendency to put myself at fault. How could they still believe Will? I missed my weekly phone calls with Anita, and despite what happened, I wished Rob was still in my life too.

The shopping dates I used to have at The Galleria in Houston with my aunt, uncle, Anita, and Rob were my favorite part of vacation growing up. My uncle and I had a tradition that we would sneak off to the Tollhouse store while the rest of the family was shopping in Saks with my aunt. Getting a special treat, like a cookie or piece of cake, that no one else in the family received bonded me with him.

"Neesha, do you want to head to the food court?" my uncle would ask me once we were bored of looking at high heels with Anita and my aunt.

"Yes!"

"Wait, can I come?" Anita would ask.

"Yeah, sure," I said with a frown.

"Well, actually, it's our tradition. Don't worry Anita, we'll only be a few minutes, then we'll be right back. Come on, Neesha."

"Are you sure?" I asked my uncle.

"No, no, Anita; it's their thing," my aunt insisted. "Let's just keep shopping. Go ahead, guys!"

Smiling, I turned to my uncle as he nodded toward the exit. "Thanks," I said to my aunt.

"Okay, Neesha, what kind of cookies are we getting this time? Chocolate chip or oatmeal?"

"Obviously, chocolate chip. Oatmeal? Way too healthy!"

"I agree!" he would joke. I thought our relationship could never be broken, and my visits to Houston had always ensured that.

Before New Year's, I was truly thankful for my family—for my parents and for my aunt, uncle, and cousins. But now, in the wake of that night, I felt no appreciation for any of them. My parents and I were fighting constantly, and I hated that they were still trying to pull me into a legal case. I did not want to think about Houston anymore, and even though they might have thought it was the right thing for me, I didn't want any part of it. My dad and I no longer spoke in the car to or from school. I grabbed my breakfast and lunch on the way out the door, and I overheard them talking about how distant I had become, how I was isolating myself.

We were beginning to fall apart. I couldn't pretend like everything was okay and try to be part of a happy family again. I didn't want them on my team, especially since they never asked me if I wanted this. Before New Year's, I would spend Sundays getting brunch with my parents, and we'd go grocery shopping after, where I could pick out any snacks I wanted. However, my visits to Barnes and Noble in elementary school with my dad were the activity I missed the most, and they were the reason English became my favorite subject.

On one particular Friday afternoon in November 2002, fall rain fell outside as I walked through the children's section of the bookstore in awe. I picked up *Stargirl*, *The Secret Garden*, and *Harry Potter* before sitting down in a yellow chair. Once half an hour passed, my dad appeared at the top of the escalator with a few books in his arms, signaling me to head to the register.

"Neesha, you ready?" he asked. "Do you have all the books you want?"

"Yes, Dad. I'm ready! Let me just grab these."

"You can choose as many books as you want on Fridays as long as you never stop reading," he said.

Everything was so simple then. Never did I think my love for anyone in my family would change, but I couldn't let my anger go. My dad's reminder that my mom and uncle were not talking both broke my heart and infuriated me.

One evening in the middle of February, I walked into the living room after my mom and I had just gotten in an argument about dinner. In a rage my dad told me, "Neesha, you are being completely out of line to your mother! You don't need to get in a fight with us every damn day."

"I'm sorry." I scoffed.

"No, you're not. You are being so bitchy all of a sudden. Why are you taking this out on everyone?"

"What?"

"Look, I know it's not your fault, but you are the reason your mom is not talking to her brother, and it is killing her. This is killing her."

I ran to my room before I let a tear fall. He had no right to blame this on me after my family in Houston already did. I was already trying to forgive myself, but this only forced me to blame myself again. Was I responsible for everything?

As February continued, I lost almost all interest in talking to my friends on the phone and focused my time on myself. I received texts from Emma asking if I was okay and from Jane seeing if I wanted to hang out. The sweetest texts came from Brad, who just wanted to be able to tease and joke with me again. He would make inside jokes about our teachers or the latest gossip. I tried laughing, but it just wasn't the same. I absorbed myself in my afternoon runs and my nonstop thoughts about food to take my mind off the legal case. Becoming more and more obsessed with the online blogs, I calculated my weight and constantly compared myself to the girls who would post pictures of their weight loss. I began to convince myself that anything I ate would make my stomach feel sick. I wanted a permanent stomachache. If I had that, then I could focus on that pain—the pain I thought I deserved.

My weight was in the mid-eighties at the beginning of March, and it was getting progressively harder to lower. My face felt stretchy, almost like Silly Putty. I noticed a couple of small, dark spots on my forehead, but I didn't know what they were. Without a second thought, I rejoiced in the ability to change how I looked. The less conventionally pretty I appeared, the less afraid I would be of something bad happening again.

But as much as I focused on distracting myself, reality had a way of showing up just as I found a moment of satisfaction. My mom told me that the detective was going to call me again on a Thursday morning in the first week of March.

I was about to get another reminder of that night. Why would I tell a stranger something I could not tell my mom? Why did she think I would be okay with telling this detective? I imagined what I would say to my parents if I had the courage to tell them that I just wanted it all to go away, but I felt ashamed. Why couldn't they just let it go and let me go back to living my life normally, with no case?

I stayed home from school that Thursday to wait for the call. Sitting on the couch in the family room, I watched the morning episode of *30-Minute Meals* while sipping on green tea. When the phone rang, I let my mom answer it. A moment later, she walked into the room and held the phone out to me with a sad face. Without meeting her eyes, I took it.

"Hello, Neesha," the detective's familiar voice said as I placed the phone to my ear.

I walked briskly down the hall to my room and slammed the door behind me. "Hi."

"I still have many questions I need to ask you about New Year's Eve.

The majority of the information I have received is from your mom, but I still need to hear it from you. We've interviewed the two boys, and they said you were the one who was instigating the events with Will the night of New Year's Eve, and he blamed this on you. But this is not the story your mom gave me, and I really need you to talk to me here."

He continued with endless questions about the different versions of our stories, but all of a sudden, I was short of breath.

I didn't raise my hand; don't call on me, I thought to myself. I sat there, mostly silent, with my left foot shaking compulsively.

"It's imperative for me to know if he made you have sex with him. I need to hear these details from you, not your mom. She is confused about the events."

Letting out a gasp of air as my heart stopped, I answered, "Look, I really don't want to do this. I don't want to talk about it, but no one had sex. Will made me give him...give him...oral sex."

Saying those words out loud shattered me.

"Was Mark in the room?"

"Yeah."

"What happened with him?"

Oh my god. "Um...he fingered me."

"Neesha, that would be considered rape. I know that is hard to hear, but it is a form of rape."

I shut my eyes as hard as I could but only saw the color red. It represented the deepest rage a girl could have.

"I have been looking into this case, and since the two boys have such a different story than you do, we would have to take it to court. It would be hard to ensure that they get prosecuted because the case would be very he-said/she-said, which judges are wary of—some don't even want to touch these kinds of cases."

"Yeah. Thanks," I said, as I hung up the phone in resignation.

My heart sank as I contemplated whether or not I really wanted to fight this case. I thought to myself that I should give this a try for the sake of my parents. After all, my mom had been talking about it for weeks. She just wanted to see those boys in jail. I remembered that she and her brother weren't speaking and how it was my fault. I could do it for her. I could be selfless and do something for her.

But these ideas vanished as I thought about encountering the two boys again. I imagined Will's memorable eyes and bit my bottom lip until I felt my teeth practically touch. Fear clouded my mind as droplets of sweat fell instead of tears. Looking down, drops of perspiration turned the white carpet gray before drying minutes later. Then a red one landed, and for a moment I felt contentment. I crawled toward my full-length mirror to see my face and noticed the blood on my lip. Licking it off to make it go away, I tasted hatred.

17 ∘ *loathe, loathe, loathe*
march - april, 2006

March became the month I started to panic about food. I didn't want to be around it. Whenever I sat in the kitchen, I grew uneasy to the point that I would have to leave. Hiding in my room became my new pastime just so I could avoid feeling restless.

The thought of seeing calorie upon calorie in front of me became overwhelming, but I didn't know how to make the fear go away. The obsession with food that started to distract me from Houston would not stop. Hoping no one had caught on, I tried to stay busy during mealtime even though every meal ended in a fight.

As I consumed myself in this mania, it became a constant battle. I would go online for at least two or three hours a day. I started reading other girls' stories about what they ate that day and if they messed up their diets. I felt stronger than the other girls on the Internet who might have broken down and eaten pizza or ice cream. I found satisfaction in knowing my self-restraint was better than theirs.

But every time the lights went out and night fell, my memories of New Year's still worried me. I started feeling more and more distant from my violated body and my broken mind. They did not feel like mine anymore, and I was not sure how to change that. I hoped to forgive myself for what happened, but my family made it harder with the constant reminders. As much as I tried to listen to the thoughts in my head that told me it was not my fault, I still thought it was.

At the end of March, I went into my bathroom on Sunday morning and examined my underwear. I searched for the blood that was supposed to be on my blue-and-white boy shorts, but it wasn't there. Confused and worried, I told myself my missed period was a fluke and waited for the next day.

Nothing.

I checked each morning that week, but I had no period. I knew this wasn't normal, since I had been getting my period consistently each month for almost a year. For a moment, I felt like I was thirteen again and it gratified me. Feeling a sense of satisfaction, as if I was pure, it stopped the clock. I had successfully destroyed my body enough to make myself that kid again. I channeled my own innocence to rewind what I saw in the mirror.

The sudden loss of my period gave me hope. I was able to change my body to the point of stopping a natural occurrence. And no one knew but me. It gave me power to see a victory like this, to see myself as I used to be even if no one else knew. It was my own secret.

But I started to develop bizarre fascinations with the pain I felt, almost wanting to cause more. I would wear rubber bands on my wrists and snap them to distract me whenever I had memories of Houston. If I felt pain on my wrist, it would take away the deeper agony that ate me up.

At the beginning of April, Jane and I went over to Emma's house to have a sleepover, something I had avoided since getting back from Houston. All week I tried to figure out how I was going to get out of eating in front of them. I thought about throwing away the food or flushing it down the toilet, but I didn't think they would get in a fight with me about it unlike my parents. We ate pizza for dinner, one of my old favorite foods, the frozen kind in the shape of a rectangle. Emma cut the pieces into small squares, and I ate exactly four of them. My nerves were shot as we watched *The Parent Trap*—one of my favorite movies—hoping they wouldn't say anything as they both ate nine or ten pieces without a second thought.

"That's the most I've ever seen you eat," Jane joked as I set my plate aside with shaking hands.

"Oh, please!" I laughed.

"We're just teasing!" Emma chimed in.

"So did you guys read the new *Teen Vogue*?" Jane asked.

"Yeah, I loved it," I said. "I want to go shopping for new spring clothes. When can we go?" I had no desire to look at clothes. "I feel like I haven't been to the mall in so long."

"Me neither. We need to go as soon as possible. I really want to get new jeans and maybe a new pair of shoes too," Emma said.

"I could use some new jeans too. I really love those." Jane pointed at the magazine.

"I do too. I want that sweater! Hey, what color do you guys want to use?" Emma asked as she brought out her giant bin of nail polish.

"I'll do blue and the dark green on my toes. Do you want your hot pink as usual, Neesha?"

"Um, I'll just paint them dark purple. I'm feeling up for a little change," I said as I grabbed the box.

"Okay, but let's paint our nails after dessert. I've been waiting for this cake all week! My mom made it for us. It looks super fancy, and there's a ton of frosting, which I know you love," Emma said as she smiled at me. But when she brought out the cake, I held up my hands in refusal.

"Oh, no, no. I'm really full." I smiled. "I'll just skip dessert. I ate a big lunch."

"Neesha, come on! It looks so good!" Emma insisted.

"I know. It looks amazing. I want a big piece!" Jane agreed.

"I'll just have a small one. It does look really good," I said.

As they ate their cake, I nibbled on the vanilla frosting, hoping they wouldn't say anything. They didn't, but as I painted my nails a dark shade of purple, I watched my best friends laugh the way I used to and missed being just like them. I missed my old self and went to bed wishing there was some magical button to press to make time rewind.

After sneaking into the large pantry in the kitchen the next morning, I weighed myself on Emma's scale. It read 84.5 pounds. Could have been worse, I thought. Before my parents picked me up, I joined Emma and Jane for breakfast and sipped coffee while they ate cereal.

"Oh, I'm having lunch with my parents, guys. I'll just have a cup of coffee," I lied when Emma handed me a bowl for cereal.

But being this drained, I couldn't function. I couldn't focus, and I couldn't work. I was not able to do homework the way I used to, and studying became a challenge. I could read while lying down, and occasionally I would do my homework on my bed, but I had lost my motivation. I would try to read at night, which used to be one of my favorite hobbies, but I would usually give up after a few chapters and bring my laptop down to the floor and search the blogs.

My high school had its spring play that April—*Guys and Dolls*. As a tradition, Jane, Emma, and I went every year to support Brad. He always had a lead part; he was going to be a movie star one day, after all. He would stroke his long blond hair and fix the collar of his Lacoste shirt, turning his nose up at his competition. Incredibly fit without working out, he was also perfect like Emma, but I had never realized how much I envied him until I no longer felt like the person I used to be. I now felt inferior.

Brad was a great friend, in different ways than Jane and Emma. He had an ego that was big enough for him to make anything happen. But even more than confident, Brad was hilarious. He always made me burst out laughing, even when all I wanted to do was lie down and give up on the day. I loved his sarcastic humor, the love he had for his friends, and his innocence. He never tried to be like the other guys in school who were constantly trying to impress everyone. Brad never felt like he had anything to prove. He had an immense amount of self-esteem and self-respect. He was who he was, and that was enough for him.

I was one of his closest friends, yet I was doing nothing but dragging down his seamlessly happy life. I thought I was the person I never wanted to be. I felt like a depressed failure. Brad was always one of my inspirations because he didn't care what anyone thought of him. Ever. I wanted that—and as much as I thought at times that I had the strong grace he had, I didn't.

After ditching Brad for weeks, we finally reunited during our free period. "So, I can't wait for the play. Are you excited to see it?" he asked.

"Yeah."

"Very convincing," he said in a sarcastic tone with a smile.

"No, I really am. Sorry. Tell me more about it."

"I'm only kidding. What's the matter? You're so quiet these days."

"No, I'm not. I'm just distracted."

"Well, you seem off. Anyway, the play should be really good this year. *Guys and Dolls* is one of my favorite plays and has been forever, you know, so that's a long time coming!"

"Definitely."

"The head of the theater department has been really encouraging lately. She told me how impressed she is with my dedication and stuff. I'm hoping next year I can get the lead role. No one my age ever gets it, but I'm excited to see what happens. Cross your fingers for me!"

"Yeah, I will. That's great."

"But other than that, I am so annoyed with the Geology homework this week. Have you done it yet?"

"Oh, shit. I totally forgot about that."

"Well, maybe we can get your dad to help us with it? I've been working on it for days."

"No, I really don't want to ask him. He is really pissing me off lately. I am just so freaking mad at him."

"Why? We just need to get it done—unless you've got any other suggestions."

"Brad, no! I really don't want his help on the homework!"

"Okay, okay. It's totally fine. I can just go in during our next free period and get help from Mr. Jones. I can email you about it after?"

"Thanks. I'd go with you, but I have some other stuff to do tomorrow."

"It's okay. We don't have to ask your dad. Sorry about that."

"Thank you. I just really don't want to talk to him."

"It's fine. Well, you know if you need anything, I'm always here. No matter what."

Brad always said the right thing. I wished I could let him be there for me more, but I felt distant from him now. My body might have been sitting across from my best friend, but my mind was still searching for direction. I was still trying to prove something to those two boys.

That I was stronger than them. That I was good enough.

I was still trying to tell *myself* that I was good enough and that New Year's wasn't my fault. But I could not, and I had not told myself it was okay to grow up and let it go.

Outings like going to see Brad in the school play kept me from being alone all the time, which I needed. Sometimes things seemed back to normal, and Brad, Jane, and Emma would come over to my house, or I'd go over to one of theirs once in awhile. We would never do much, just watch movies together. Funny ones like *Meet the Parents*, ones that made us laugh. I needed a good laugh, and Brad, Emma, and Jane knew it—especially Brad.

"I freaking love this movie! I think I could watch it every weekend for the rest of my life," Emma said as she held the DVD in her hands.

"Me too!" Jane agreed. "I have never gotten sick of it—"

"It's great, but we have watched it, like, a hundred times," Brad interrupted.

"Oh please, how many times have we watched your musicals?" Jane said.

"Yeah, yeah pass the popcorn!" Brad said as Jane handed him the bowl.

"Thanks. So, can we just talk about how awful Geology is these days? That's basically the hardest class I have ever taken. Well, I'm sure you two get it, but Neesha and I aren't the most brilliant when it comes to good old science. Right, Neesha?"

"It's pretty much the biggest waste of time. Science is such a joke. Why do we have to take it again? I am so over that class," I said with a little of the liveliness I used to have in my voice.

"Lord knows. It's awful!" scoffed Brad.

"Oh, it's not that bad," Emma said.

"Says the one who gets straight A's without even trying."

"Just 'cause you're jealous! Kidding, kidding," Emma joked.

"Ha. Ha. Oh please, I will pass the class! Plus, who needs that stuff in life anyway?"

"I mean we do have college ahead. We might have to take science then."

"That's enough lecturing, Emma. Can you bring the pizza over here? I'm really hungry tonight. Oh, the chips too!" Brad said as she brought them over from the kitchen.

"So, I loved you in the play this year! It was such a good show. You were amazing as always!" Jane said.

"Aw, thank you! That is so sweet. I loved acting in it, but I'm kind of relieved it's over so I can have my life back. Rehearsals every single day—what a drag!"

"That sounds like such a snooze," Emma said.

"You with the little comments!" Brad threw a piece of popcorn at Emma with a big smile on his face.

"I'm joking!"

"Food fight!" Brad yelled.

The four of us would plan a movie night at one of our houses every Saturday night, but as much as I wished things would go back to normal, I rarely ended up attending. They insisted and insisted, but I lost interest knowing there would be popcorn, chips, and my favorite candies there.

When I did actually make it to a movie night, my dad would drive me while I would listen to my iPod. I think he was sick of arguing every night, and he no longer knew what to do. I sat there staring out the window on the rides to Jane's house. We would usually stop and pick up Brad because his house was on the way. During our rides, I noticed my dad's jaw clenching. I had built up a never-ending wall between him and me.

Then on one ride home, he surprised me. "Neesha, you know your mom and I are always here for you?"

"I know," I said as I swallowed tears.

"We're only concerned about you, and I want you to know it's okay to be sad about what happened in Houston. I mean I even cried about it, and your mother hasn't stopped. It's hard on all of us." He glanced at me while I nodded. "But really, I know you're probably trying to deal with it on your own, but you need to make this easier on your mother. She is falling apart."

My parents had always been a team my whole life, and this was no different. If I was ever in a fight with one of them, they always took each other's side. I knew he wanted me to understand that he wanted us to get over this together, but I just could not do it. I could not forgive him for blaming me for my mom and uncle not talking, and I could not forgive them for forcing this case on me. The pain was too deep. Just as deep as the pain in the conversations that I didn't want to have with the detective. My dad just did not get it.

"Yeah, I'll try," I said as I rolled my eyes behind my sunglasses and turned up my iPod.

18 ∘ *growing colder*
may - june, 2006

I thought I was winning my game of running away from that night. But I wasn't. I had put all my concentration and energy into not eating to avoid what I needed to overcome, but deep down I felt agitated. In May, all those months later, I would still lie down at night and see the boys' faces while I tossed and turned.

I constantly attempted to convince myself that I was still the person before New Year's, yet I didn't know who that was anymore. After all, my pink tank top fit me now. Didn't that make me the girl I wanted to be again? I thought I was winning. But as much as I tried to tell myself this, I knew I had not forgiven myself.

I was planning to take driver's education in the middle of June, and I hoped that my parents would still let me even though I hadn't kept up the 3.0 GPA they wanted me to have. My classes had lost all meaning to me; my GPA was at a 2.9 when I should have been excelling. I knew I had more potential than this, but I didn't have the energy to go to class and apply myself. I felt like I was wasting my parents' money in private school because I was only going through the motions. I was struggling, but I felt like I was too consumed to save myself. Nor did I want to.

The day my report card came, I begged and pleaded telling my parents that I would bring my GPA up the next semester, if I could only take the driver's education class. "I promise! Come on, I'm sorry. I know I could have done better, but I mean these classes were awful." I cried in the kitchen with my hands clasped in front of me. "I just didn't do well this semester because my classes were really hard. Mom, please. I promise I will do better next year. I swear!"

"Neesha, you have really let us down this semester," my mom scolded. She sat at the table, worried lines crossing her face. "You aren't a part of this family anymore, you look sick all the time, and you clearly cannot live up to our expectations. I don't think you should be driving. Driving is a privilege, and you haven't been holding up your end of the bargain."

I ignored the heartbreak on her face and her comments about who I had become, focusing all my energy instead on the issue of the driving class. "Please, Mom, I will do anything! I just want to drive! Everyone else has already taken the class."

"Neesha you have to bring up your grades. If you are even thinking about volleyball in the fall, you can't get grades like this," my dad jumped in. "But maybe you can take the class. It's just a class. Plus she has the appointment with Dr. Young on Monday anyway," he said to my mom.

"Oh my god! Who's Dr. Young?"

My mom glanced at my dad, and then she looked at me and sighed. "We made an appointment with a therapist for you. We're really worried about you, and we are not going to sit here and watch you distance yourself and go on these ridiculous runs every day. We just won't. You're going to go. You can take the class—but even if you scream and cry about the appointment, you're still going."

"What?"

"Neesha, don't talk back to your mom. Dr. Young specializes in this stuff. Also, you have to start eating at the table with us again! I will not get in any more fights about this. You eating in your room is not going to happen anymore. We gave you a chance to prove yourself in school and you didn't. Changes need to be made starting now. Neesha, this is already decided. You're going on Monday," My dad said, looking me right in the eyes. But I walked out of the room before I could hear the last part.

Monday came and I arrived at Dr. Young's office. I took a seat in the waiting room. Her office was on the second level of a brown office building, up ten steep stairs. The fancy royal blue couches in the waiting room looked like they should be in a tearoom in London. Books rested on the table with titles such as *Beating Bulimia* or *How I Beat Compulsive Eating*. I scoffed as I waited, looking down at the hardwood floor.

That first visit set a pattern for what every visit was like. After waiting for Dr. Young to call my name, I would go into her office and take a seat on the giant brown couch, which was far too large for any person to be comfortable in. I would sit there usually in baggy sweatpants or my biggest jeans, a T-shirt, and a hoodie or sweater. I found myself wearing my pink Abercrombie tank top more and more often underneath all my clothes, which would typically be about three or four layers of shirts and jackets.

My therapist was a middle-aged woman named Miranda Young. She had long brownish-blonde hair and was about five foot eight. She wore black glasses, a fancy blouse, and always a pencil skirt. Every time I would go into her office, she would make a comment about what I was wearing—"Cute shirt!" or "You look comfortable." I was never able to decipher what she meant by these remarks, but I just knew they annoyed me.

Her questions were ridiculous: "What is your goal weight?" "How many calories do you eat a day?"

Like I would tell her any of those things.

I told her that I didn't know any of these answers because I didn't count calories.

Lie.

I told her that I didn't really weigh myself.

Lie.

I told her that I just went on jogs here and there.

Lie.

I told her my parents and I just weren't getting along because of school stuff.

Lie.

I told her that I had a consistent period every month.

Lie.

Because I didn't trust this woman, therapy was difficult. And I wasn't willing to change my ways for her. I knew she couldn't change me and make me forgive myself. After every question, I feared that she would tell my parents the answers even though she swore she wouldn't.

She tried to establish a friendship with me during that first visit by asking me what music I liked, which I thought was the worst psychological technique a therapist could possibly use. I mean, yes, she was doing her job, but I thought I was so much smarter than this woman. I thought she should actually experience what happened over New Year's before she passed judgment on me. I hated her constant analysis as she vigorously jotted down notes. What was she writing? What was she saying about me?

She couldn't relate to my situation or me—no one could. She asked why I started losing the weight, but I sat there silently. Telling this therapist what those boys did that night wouldn't make me feel any better. Why would I tell a stranger anything about that?

I wasn't going to fix myself for her. I wasn't going to fix myself for my parents. I wasn't going to fix myself for those two boys. My wrecked body was there to stay, and I wasn't seeking a bandage to put it back together by talking to this woman. Starvation was how I was fixing myself—not for anyone else, only for *myself*.

Each Monday afternoon made me squirm and sweat, for those forty-five minutes, at least, I froze on that couch. Dr. Young told me that if I wouldn't talk, we would sit in silence together.

Really excellent psychological technique, I thought to myself. *Truly. Top notch.*

I hated this woman.

I was quite confident that most fourteen-year-olds would hate going to a shrink if they had no desire to get better. If I were really ready to forgive myself, maybe it would have been different. But all I wanted was to fall further and further away.

She claimed that she wasn't trying to make me eat. She repeatedly told me, "I'm not telling you to change your habits. I am not here to make you gain weight."

I didn't buy it.

She would ask me about my parents and my best friends. I told her that my best friend was Emma and left Brad and Jane out of it.

She asked me what we did together, and I explained that we would mostly watch movies. She asked me what my favorite movie was and if we would eat during the movies.

"You know," she said, smiling, "snacks?"

Yes, I know what the word *snacks* means.

Question after question.

Oh my god, will it ever end?

I thought that I hid my weight of 83 pounds extremely well beneath my layers of clothing. But Dr. Young pressed me incessantly, asking about my childhood and why I felt the need to lose weight. I blew her off, telling her that everything was fine. My childhood was fine. There were no problems then and no problems now. But I didn't even put effort into making up a good lie or sounding convincing. We both knew something was wrong, or else I wouldn't be sitting on that giant couch having these discussions.

I had no desire to change, but most of all, I had no desire to talk about what happened to change my entire life. These sessions angered me more than they amused me. Tempted to push her chair over, I squeezed my hands in my hooded jacket as hard as I could. I bit my lip and sat there silently staring at the black clock hanging on the wall.

Why did I have to talk to this woman? Why did I have to tell her anything about myself? I felt like I owed her nothing, and that was exactly what she was going to get. Every minute in this office felt like a minute underwater, and I just needed to come up for air.

I would not tell her that I was doing this to escape the terror those two boys still gave me. Living in fear had become exhausting but normal. I now ran away from myself. I ran away from Houston and those boys. I fell silent when she asked me why I thought I was doing this to myself. The answer I gave her was that I didn't know.

She continued her buddy-buddy techniques for the next few months that I sat on that couch. I spent most of our sessions daydreaming and staring out the window at the Sandia Mountains, thinking about how this was the only view I enjoyed in Albuquerque. I would stare at the mountains and imagine myself standing at the top looking down at the world, feeling invincible and being free of the adults trying to dictate my life. Free of Dr. Young, the detective, and my parents. But most of all free of the boys who still haunted me.

Why did I have to continue to talk? Why did I have to tell all these people anything about my life? Especially the most private things that were none of their business. Their interfering never fucking ended. Would I ever catch a break?

I would never tell Dr. Young what happened in Houston, and I would never tell my parents either. I couldn't tell my mom what happened when I got back, so why did she think I would be okay with telling anyone else? Shame still overwhelmed me, and I could not even imagine being happy again. It felt impossible.

19 ∘ *drive*
june, 2006

Driver's Education finally arrived, and the thought of getting my permit was one of the things that gave me the hope of freedom. However, the patience and responsibility that came with it overwhelmed me. I had a terrible attitude, but I dreamt of the morning drives where I could have a moment of solitude. It didn't scare me until I began watching the videos they showed in class — the ones where teenagers ended up in car wrecks and their dead bodies fell out onto the street.

My classes were twice a week for three weeks, and luckily Jane was in there with me. I hadn't seen her in a while, with school ending and summer beginning. Since she lived so close, her mom would pick me up on the way and drive us together while we would have our own quiet conversation in the backseat. I wondered if her mom noticed Jane was now doing most of the talking, even though a year ago I would have been.

"Hey Neesha, how's your summer going?" her mom would ask.

"It's good, how about you?"

"Good. Are you looking forward to the volleyball season starting back up soon? Big year — sophomore year!"

"I can't wait," I lied. I had not even thought about the season in months, but it had always been my favorite sport, and I held out hope of being involved on the team the way that I used to be.

Driver's Ed started in the late morning on Tuesdays and Thursdays, so I would take a yogurt and protein bar, making sure my parents saw it when I waved goodbye, strolling out of my house with a grin on my face. I would arrive at class and throw the food away once I walked into the building. So clever. I would toss it in the bathroom trash so Jane wouldn't catch on. I thought these tricks out carefully, but I didn't think anyone actually knew the little lies I would tell in order to make it through the day.

On the second day, Jane blatantly asked me, "Neesha, are you doing okay? You seem so tiny. And you're wearing a sweater in the middle of the summer. What's going on?"

"You know, I'm always cold. Nothing's going on," I'd say in an arrogant tone. Why would she think it was appropriate to ask me about that? It was so annoying.

Sitting through the class for three hours, my body was starting to punish me for what I was putting it through. My exhausted neck grew tired of holding my head up. Massaging the back of my neck, I felt my protruding spine. Feeling the bones comforted me. After class, my dad usually picked us up, and we'd stop at Starbucks. I would get black coffee with three Splendas and acted like I poured in milk to trick Jane and my dad. I don't think I was fooling anyone.

Conceited and proud, I would say "goodbye" and "thanks" when we would drop Jane off at her house. Sometimes I saw her little brothers, who seemed to look at me differently, almost like they didn't know me anymore, but I would just wave as we drove away. Once we parked in the garage, I immediately rushed inside to take a nap, giving in to my exhaustion.

The hunger pains didn't satisfy me like they used to. Once I woke up from my nap, I gulped down a bottle a Diet Coke and ate a protein bar. I enjoyed the bar like it was a three-course meal as I changed into my running clothes. It had become repetitive, and once I returned from my run, I chugged a bottle of water and ate a snack in front of my mom.

She said, "Neesha, you are really running way too much. You need to eat more than an apple. Let me make you a sandwich."

"Fine," I'd snap and take the sandwich to my room. Sometimes I would eat the sandwich because I was so hungry. Failure. I would avoid conversation with her and get on my computer to look at the blogs.

It was an inescapable routine that had become a way of life.

The tough part came once Driver's Education ended in June. I needed fifty hours of driving with an adult, but I only ended up driving two hours that summer. I had no desire to do the actual practice with my dad because the stress of being in a car with him as his jaw clenched enraged me. I had no patience; I was only irritable. It especially bothered me when he told me how to do something specific or when he corrected me on something that I was doing wrong. The two times I did try to drive with him we spent the entire hour in a parking lot trying to right-turn and serpentine.

What a disaster.

"What are you doing!" my dad would shout when I made a mistake, such as not checking my mirror before turning. As his jaw would clench, I'd lose my temper and begin screaming at him.

"Dad, what? I'm trying here, and you're really stressing me out!"

"You need to look in your mirror first!"

"Don't yell. I will do it! Oh my god!" I yelled back.

"Neesha, you aren't listening to anything I'm saying. Driving is unbelievably dangerous. You have a thousand-pound weapon, and you could kill someone. Why are you being so difficult, anyway? What the hell has gotten into you?"

"Oh my god, forget this. I don't want to do this anyway!"

I ended both of those lessons red in the face from our screaming matches.

I gave up on driving after that. I decided I'd rather sit in the car and listen to my iPod while someone else drove me, zoning out like I had been doing since January. I was not willing to change any of my habits.

20 ∘ *birthdays*
july, 2006

July used to be my favorite month. Summers before this one were filled with afternoon runs and volleyball with the team at school. I especially loved July because open gym nights—where anyone can come play—took place every Tuesday and Thursday. The summer scrimmages I had attended in middle school allowed me to get involved with the older girls and play the sport that I believed I was born to play. I used to be a leader—the setter who had been playing for three years, the most agile girl on the team, the one who could save any ball that came over the net.

My parents had forced me to stop running outside because Dr. Young said it wasn't a good idea. But ending my outdoor workouts were for the best because my body tensed up against the pavement, making me feel stiff and dysfunctional. The conversation with my father turned into an argument, naturally, but we came to an agreement. As an alternative, my dad bought me a gym membership, and I started to go to the Sports and Wellness Gym with him. The summer afternoons consisted of my dad driving me to the gym. During the year, he would go every morning after he dropped me off at school; now he just moved his workout to the afternoon. He didn't mind rearranging his schedule for me even though I was ungrateful.

The gym visits allowed me to do my runs on the treadmill and not deal with the outdoors. Watching the burned calories go up as I ran, I found comfort in the burn that stung my legs. It was something I was now used to and still gave me the satisfaction that I might have found a way to distract myself from the guilt consuming me from New Year's.

There were times when I would look around the gym and find the room was spinning, but then it began to feel good, a sign that I was seeing results. Even though the car rides forced me to talk to my dad, they were worth it, as I was able to burn off so many extra calories.

"Look, we need to talk about volleyball..." he said one warm afternoon on the ride to the gym. "I know you love it, but we don't think you should be working out so hard. You are already exerting yourself way too much. I know you want to, but your mom and I just aren't going to allow you to exercise so much. Dr. Young says it could be really bad for your health too."

"What? I can't believe you're taking this from me!" I growled. "This is such a joke! Why would she say that?"

"Neesha, no one is trying to punish you. It's just really bad for you, and you haven't been eating more or being any nicer to your mom. And we all know beneath all the sweatpants and sweatshirts you wear, you're barely there."

"What are you talking about? I've always been small. This is so ridiculous!"

"You have become so distant and never seem to be here. I need you to help me understand what you need. Your mom doesn't even know what to do for you anymore because all you do is yell at her. So you need to start being a hell of a lot nicer to her. I told you about this before, and you haven't changed."

"Whatever. I don't want to talk about it."

"I know your birthday is coming up, and it's your favorite day of the year, so why don't we use this opportunity to start over for all of us?"

"Yeah, sure," I muttered before turning up the volume on my iPod.

For my fifteenth birthday on July 27, my parents told me that I could invite my friends to the Olive Garden for dinner. They said Emma, Brad, Jane, and I could sit at our own table, and they would be at a different one. Hesitant to eat in front of my friends, I knew I had to pull it together for this dinner, not only for them, but also for myself. I could be happy for a day, couldn't I? Aside from New Year's Eve, there was no other day I loved more than my birthday, and they all knew that. My parents knew I always counted down to this day, and deep down I was excited even though I knew I would have to pretend like I was the person before Houston.

But one thing was missing though. Anita was always the first one to call me and wish me a happy birthday, but she hadn't called me since January. Before leaving for dinner, my parents gave me my present, which almost made up for Anita's silence. I undid the white ribbon and opened the blue box to find a heart necklace with the letters *N.A.* engraved on it.

"We wanted to give you a gift that matched my necklace," my mom said with a sigh, clearly holding back tears. "And now that you're fifteen, we want you to know we are proud of you and we love you so much. We know you're going through a hard time, but we're here for you."

"Thanks, Mom," I whispered as I tried not to cry.

My dad pulled the necklace out of the box and then put it on my neck while I held my hair to one side, though I didn't want him to see how bony my neck had become. He squeezed my shoulders, and for a moment we bonded the way we used to. But then fear overwhelmed me, and I desperately tried to keep my distance so he couldn't feel my back covered in three layers of clothing.

Walking into the restaurant, I saw my friends waiting with open arms. "Happy Birthday!" they all exclaimed at once.

"Thanks," I spoke with excitement. I tried to tell myself to relax and have a good time, but instead I remained cold.

The hostess called my name, and we all walked to our two tables. After sitting down, I refused to take my blue sweater off even though everyone else was wearing sundresses and shorts. My paper-thin skin and brittle bones couldn't take the chilly temperature in this restaurant.

Everyone ordered pasta, fettuccine Alfredo, or spaghetti, but I ordered soup. I looked at the table as everyone was drawing on the white paper over the white tablecloth. My friends laughed, but I simply sat there. I tried to smile at Emma when she gave me a look of concern, but it was just too hard. I remembered the year before, celebrating with Anita, and it broke my heart that I couldn't share holidays with her anymore. I took a couple of gulps of Diet Coke and tried to put on a smile. However, the absence of my family saddened me.

We finished dinner, and my parents drove the four of us back to my house to have birthday cake. It used to be my favorite dessert and the best part of my birthday. I would even celebrate my half birthday sometimes just to have one. But this year, fear fell over me when I looked at my birthday cake. Vanilla layers covered with pink whipped-cream frosting. There were pink and white flowers on top; it reminded me of a little girl's cake. A child's cake. One I had when I turned seven. But I wasn't a child anymore, not after Houston.

I thought I needed a different dessert, one with black crows instead of pink roses. I wished that I could enjoy a piece with my best friends and parents, but the thought was so farfetched — so impossible — that it almost made me scoff.

They all sang "Happy Birthday" to me as I faked a smile and nodded along. I blew out my candles, wishing to turn back the clock to my fourteenth birthday and do it all over. My mom sliced the cake, and then we took our plates into the sunroom. I pushed my fork around as Jane and Emma laughed at Brad's jokes, but I felt shaky just looking at the calorie-rich dessert. Finally, I swallowed the saliva in my mouth, took a breath, and ate a bite. Then two, then four, then eight, then the whole piece. Remembering how much I loved this sweet treat, I couldn't stop myself.

As time passed and the night grew late, I could feel the pink cake sitting in the bottom of my stomach. Jane and Emma's parents picked them up, leaving Brad and me alone in the sunroom. We talked about the movie we watched together the weekend before. I smiled at him, one of the innocent smiles that fifteen-year-olds give to boys when they are truly joyful—truly happy—which I was in that moment and hadn't been in months.

"Neesha, I hope you had a good birthday," he told me softly after a smile. He blushed and looked down at his hands. "You really mean a lot to me. I hope you know that."

"Thanks, Brad," I answered. My heartbeat was speeding up, but whether it was from the over analysis of the calories in the cake or something else, I wasn't sure. "You're one of the best friends I could ask for. Thanks for coming. I'm sorry things have been so off this year. I know I'm completely different, and everything is a total mess…but…"

He nodded, and then he leaned in closer to me. With his nose now a few inches from mine, I realized he was trying to kiss me. But when I looked into his eyes, I didn't see Brad.

I saw Will.

I put my hands on Brad's chest and shoved him away from me. With no warning I started sobbing.

"What's the matter?" he asked, eyes wide.

"Nothing." I stood, shaking all over, and headed for the door. "I just can't do this. I can't…"

"Neesha," he called after me as I stood up to run away. "Wait— Neesha, I'm sorry!"

I ran to my room without bothering to say goodbye. I glimpsed at his parents by the front door, and I knew I had to at least say something, despite my racing heart.

"Happy birthday, Neesha!" his mom said.

"Thank you!"

"How was it? How does it feel to be fifteen?"

"It's great. I feel much older and wiser, you know…"

She laughed. "Well, you're a beautiful girl, Neesha, and you're going to be great. I hope this is the best year for you yet."

"Thank you so much. That means a lot. I actually have to run, but Brad's on his way."

I sprinted back to my room, and Brad left with his mom. Lying on my floor, full and pained, I just kept thinking of Will's eyes. I thought about his face being close to mine and how the heat of his body warmed mine. I thought of the smells in that exercise room. The bitter, putrid smells. The smells of me and the smells of him. The smells of our naked bodies.

I hated those smells.

As I lay on the ground, I couldn't shake my feelings. I needed to do something. I had lost all my trust in Brad for trying to kiss me. He was the only boy I had really let into my life, but that was over. Now he scared me more than anything. I couldn't think of him even hugging me.

I would never be able to trust him again. Why would he try to kiss me?

Not wanting to think about how I now hated one of my best friends, I quickly jumped to worrying about how to get the piece of cake out of my body. I ran to the bathroom and looked at my round face. I had never made myself throw up before, but now I thought I had to. It was imperative that the food leave my body that instant.

I went over to the toilet and bent over. The smell of the toilet water disgusted and nauseated me. I looked at that porcelain bowl and thought about getting the calories out of my body. I stuck the two fingers of my right hand down my throat and coughed painfully. I made a loud gagging noise as my body shot forward.

Nothing.

But I tried again.

My stomach felt like someone punched the inside of it, but all that food was still in there. I stuck my fingers down farther and rubbed the back of my throat. The cake came up suddenly, pink and bittersweet in the toilet bowl.

I kept going.

The soup started to come up, a sour taste that I had no desire to ever experience again. Tears rushed into my eyes as I stood up. My fingers were full of pink vomit and wet spit. I immediately washed them and brushed my teeth to get the acid taste to go away. I stared at myself in the mirror, eyes red, crying. My face was swollen and puffy like a plum; it looked like I had eaten a bag of potato chips and poured an entire shaker of salt on them. Almost like I'd gained twenty pounds. Where did my cheekbones go?

I forced myself to calm down and tried to catch my breath, thinking about how much effort that had taken.

I never wanted to throw up again. And I wouldn't.

I went to bed with the worst stomachache I had ever had while tossing and turning racked with guilt over throwing up. The taste of vomit still in my mouth made me feel like I was rotting, and seeing it made me more ashamed of myself than ever before. Ashamed to be heard or even seen, I was now ashamed to be in the same room as other people. As acid bubbled in my stomach, I felt ashamed to be me.

21 ○ *sleeping less and less*
august, 2006

July finally turned into August, and the habits I consumed myself in were impossible to stop. I was sticking to eating just my safe foods, but even if I tried to eat what my parents made for dinner, fear overwhelmed me in a way it never had before. These foods were the only ones I would have in front of my parents unless they forced me into eating a sandwich or fish. Late at night, when no one was awake, I would usually break down and go into the kitchen alone. I stared at everything in the refrigerator imagining what I would eat if I could eat anything.

My life was full of obsessions. Spending an hour in the kitchen at night, I would read every label on the packages, from crackers to soup cans to how many calories were in a bag of potato chips, which used to be my favorite snack, but I hadn't eaten any in months. Once I went through everything I could find, I would usually eat two or three slices of bread. I would even toast them and put a little bit of sugar-free strawberry jelly on each slice. Maybe a bowl of cereal without milk, or if I was desperate and felt like I had to eat something more, I might have a couple spoonfuls of peanut butter, stopping once I felt guilty.

One evening I heard my mom talking to my dad in the hall. "She's barely there. This is seriously getting out of hand, and Dr. Young just keeps saying that it's going to take time to get her back to normal."

"I know, but what else can we possibly do? She's going, and I mean…that's all we can do. Don't be so hard on yourself."

"Yes, but I'm just getting frustrated because she won't even eat with us, and I don't know how much more of this I can take. And her attitude is unbelievable."

After hearing that, I wanted to get out of my house as soon as I could. They did not understand what I had gone through and the fact that I could not escape this mess. I used to love family dinners with my parents, but now I couldn't stand them. I didn't know how to fix this. I wished there was a switch I could flip to transform me back into the girl I used to be. I really did. I didn't want to be this person, but I didn't know how to be me anymore, and that scared me the most. I used to be funny and loved my parents more than anything, but now we were in two different worlds.

The summer was ending, and I was actually a little relieved to go back to school because it made not eating easier to hide without the watchful eyes of my parents. I still had a few weeks left before school started, and I was trying really hard to avoid back-to-school shopping for clothes. I tried to tell my mom that I didn't need any—and really, I didn't. Everything still fit from the year before. I mean, hell, all my clothes were too big. Nevertheless, my mom got her way, and we went to the mall together.

The mirrors at the store were my worst nightmare.

Once we arrived at the mall, I told her I only wanted to go to Abercrombie—the one for kids. The same place where I bought my tank top in Houston, the store that actually made me feel like the person I used to be. Plus, I knew all the clothes because I'd visit their website when I was online. I knew every advertisement, every sweater, all the pairs of jeans they had, and which hoodies were the cutest. I raced around the store, trying to make the trip as fast as possible, and I picked up a couple of shirts randomly. I chose everything in a size large this time. Even though I knew I weighed only 83.5 pounds, I still *felt* like a large. I didn't even bother trying them on. I didn't want my mom to see me in just a T-shirt, and I didn't know how I would react in a dressing room full of mirrors. What would these mirrors make me look like?

"This one is cute!" my mom said smiling as she took one of the shirts from me, a blue blouse with plenty of fabric to hide my body. All the shirts had long sleeves; I had no desire to show my arms in Abercrombie tank tops the way I did when I bought the one in Houston. "Don't you want some dresses or maybe skirts to go with these?"

"No, I'm fine. I have plenty of jeans."

My mom frowned, then she turned down an aisle with skirts. She took a knee-length black skirt off the rack and held it up. "What about this one?"

"I'm ready to go," I said. "I'll get these shirts, and I don't really need anything else."

"Are you sure you don't need more pants or jeans?"

"I have enough, Mom, really. Plus, I don't know my size, and I just want to get out of here. Can we please just go?"

I was not going to put myself through the hell of trying on pants— like I wanted to see my body in the full-length mirror of the store.

My mom stared at me for a long moment, then she sighed heavily. "Fine, Neesha. Let's just pay for these."

On the drive home, my voice was raspy from exhaustion. "Thank you."

"You're welcome," she said stiffly. "You know you could be a little more thankful. Honestly. You're not making any effort. I wanted this to be a nice time for us to catch up, but you won't even talk to me! It hurts my feelings that you don't want to go shopping together anymore."

"Mom, let's just forget it. Thanks for the clothes."

"No, honey, this is not okay anymore. You wear the same baggy clothes every day. You don't eat. Why won't you just talk to me? You know you can tell me anything. I thought we were friends. You used to talk to me about everything. How are your friends? I haven't seen them in forever."

"They are fine. Everyone is great." I ignored the comments about my eating.

"Good, well, I would love to see them sometime. How is Brad?"

"He's fine too," I lied. I hadn't talked to him since my birthday.

"Are you excited for school?"

"Yeah, Mom, I am."

"You have a new English teacher this year. Are you looking forward to that? I know that's your favorite subject."

"Yeah, it should be an exciting year." I stared out the window and daydreamed about getting away from my mom.

I thought I was home free from fighting with my parents with the school year starting in a couple of weeks. Jane, Emma, and I had been texting a bit more, which made me feel like I was back to my old self, and we had one last sleepover before school began. We spent the whole time talking about how soccer and volleyball tryouts were coming up. Everyone knew I wanted to make the varsity team.

I had been seeing Dr. Young just like my parents wanted me to, so I thought there was no reason I wouldn't be able to try out. However, the week before school started, my parents called me into the kitchen and told me we needed to talk. That was never a good sign.

"We know you are starting school next week, Neesha," my dad began, "but we think you still need to be seeing Dr. Young, and we don't think volleyball tryouts are the best idea, neither does Dr. Young."

"What?" I yelled. "That's ridiculous! I am fine. It's a total waste of money! And why can't I try out?"

"It's not a waste of money if it's helping you," my mom told me, her voice choked with tears.

Exhausted and desperate, I simply slumped over in my wooden chair and stared at them.

"Your grades need to come up this semester, or you won't be getting your license or driving at all, for that matter," my dad went on. "And for god's sake, you need to start eating, Neesha!"

"What are you talking about?" I shouted. "I'm fine! I eat enough! I go to the gym with you—you're there; you see my workouts! What's the problem?"

He pointed a finger at me. "You'd better watch it. If you are even considering convincing us to let you play volleyball this year, you'd better think again. You do know you need parental consent, right?"

"Jesus Christ," I muttered as I stood up and slammed the chair into the table. I retreated to my room, ignoring their commands for me to come back.

I shut the door. I fucking hate them, I said to myself.

22 ∘ *pass/set*
august, 2006

Since I didn't go to any of the open gyms that summer for volleyball, I wasn't as strong as everyone else, but also, I had barely been eating. Making varsity would be a challenge—let alone trying to convince my parents to let me play after our argument. I avoided talking about volleyball and became more pleasant for the rest of the time before school started. I ate more in front of them and tried to strike up conversations even though my parents knew I was putting on an act.

Volleyball tryouts were coming up during the first week of school. My parents knew that I didn't have the strength in my brittle bones to play the same sport I had played for years, but I was not giving up easily when fighting my dad on the topic. If I could just convince him to let me play, maybe, just maybe, I would somehow find the energy required to participate. My natural talent would be enough to earn a spot on the team.

I found my dad in the living room and sat down on the arm of the couch. "Hey Dad," I said in my cheeriest voice. "Tryouts are tomorrow. I know you don't want me to go, but I wanted to ask again because I know I will make the team."

My dad turned the volume off on the television. "No. You're not trying out, Neesha. We told you no before, and your mom and I have discussed it with Dr. Young. None of us think it's a good idea. You really do not need the exercise—you exercise too much as it is considering how little you eat. That much exertion could be dangerous with how frail you've gotten. You don't listen to any of us, and I don't know why you'd think we would let you go."

Tears began streaming down my face.

I could tell my father was uncomfortable by my burst of emotion; I had remained cold in front of my parents since January.

"I just want to play volleyball with my friends again," I whispered. "Please…all the coaches know I'm good enough, so I don't have to try very hard—I'm already on the team. I'm *always* on the team."

"You are not allowed to exercise with them," he said, his voice still firm. "I'm not letting you go."

"Please!" I screamed. "Just talk to Mom about it, okay? I don't see what the problem is here! I am completely fine!"

I stomped down the hall to my room and slammed the door. Like a child.

About an hour later, my mom came in. It was only eight o'clock in the evening, but my lights were off. "Neesha?" she asked softly. "Are you awake?"

"What do you want?" I asked beneath my sheets.

"We've decided you can go to tryouts, honey, but only the first half—the actual volleyball part. We'll let you go to the scrimmages, but you're not allowed to go to the conditioning in the afternoon. Your body does not need the weight training, but you should see your coach since you didn't get to see him all summer. I know you miss him and the team."

"Thank you," I managed to say in the darkness. I also knew those two words alone made her happy.

After waking up the next day, I didn't weigh myself. I thought I had a chance of making the team and wanted to give myself a break. I walked into the kitchen with the first real smile on my face in months.

My mom looked shocked when I entered the kitchen smiling, but she didn't say anything as I took the glass of green tea she made me and sat in my wooden chair to wait for my dad. In my volleyball gear for the first time since the year before, I felt in my element. My kneepads, a child's medium, were falling off of my knees, but I felt right. I felt like my old self.

Attempting to hide the bagginess of my gear from my mom, I wore my black sweatpants over my red cotton shorts and kneepads. I decided to eat breakfast to please her, despite my aversion to food. I needed energy for tryouts, and I felt hopeful.

I had to succeed. After all, I loved this game. It was what I did best when I was young.

I ate an apple and the oatmeal my mom made me, knowing that the oatmeal would fill me up for hours.

My mom watched me with a small, surprised smile on her face. "It's nice to see you have an appetite," she said.

I didn't say anything, but I finished eating the oatmeal. When my dad appeared in the kitchen, I waved goodbye to my mom, happy for the first time in months.

She smiled at me. "Good luck! Be careful, honey. I mean it!"

My dad, still incredibly hesitant about all this, drove me to tryouts. I tuned him out with my iPod and sipped my tea. I hopped out of the car when we pulled up to school.

"Honey," he said through his rolled-down window. His forehead was creased with worry. "You sure you're up to this?"

"Yeah, Dad," I said. Of course, I was up to it. This was my sport. My passion. "I'll see you later!"

Inside the gym I found Emma, who was trying out this year as well. She wasn't sure if she would make varsity, but I was sure I would. We started running around the gym, and I felt confident. I swung my arms with strength and opened up my stride, but my breath felt shorter than usual. Even though I had been running on the treadmill every day over the summer, this was more challenging than I'd expected. The stamina I used to have when it came to running no longer allowed me to coast. In all the years I played volleyball, running was the easiest part for me.

I could outrun anyone on the team when it came to suicides or laps around the gym, but now pressure filled my chest and I needed to slow down my pace.

After a few laps around the gym, the volleyball warm-up started. Relieved that I would not need as much endurance, I knew I could rely on my skills. But once we started passing the volleyball back and forth, I felt a cramp in my stomach. I had lost my touch! I couldn't move as fast as I could the year before! I had no agility!

"You okay, Neesha?" Emma asked me as we went through the warm-up exercises.

"Can't really breathe," I gasped, keeping a smile on my face. "But I'm fine."

She caught the ball and set it down at her feet, shaking her head. "Let me get you some water, okay?"

"Emma! No, I'm fine!"

But before I could protest, she ran off. I rolled my eyes and headed in the opposite direction. Going outside for some air, I wanted to avoid anyone seeing me, especially the coaches.

I took a few breaths in the hot summer heat and closed my eyes. Get it together, Neesha. You have to do better than this if you're going to play. Don't lose this, too.

I went back into the gym and drank the water Emma silently handed me. We started a drill with the other thirty girls who were there to try out. I knew them all from the team and from school. I had been on junior varsity the year before but was pulled up to varsity freshman year for the state championships, so I knew I would make the varsity squad. But as I began running, I thought I was going to throw up from dizziness. I welcomed the feeling at first—it used to comfort me when it hit me on the treadmill—but after a moment, I realized this was different. The queasiness made the room spin. A clammy sweat broke out on my skin, and my knees felt stiff. Get it together! I told myself.

"*Mine!*" I yelled as I went to set the ball and jogged to the back of the line. I placed my hands over my head.

Emma appeared beside me suddenly. "Neesha! Are you okay?"

"Yeah, I'm fine!"

But when I jumped up to set the next ball, I felt a tiny pop in my ankle as I fell down to land on the wood floor. Not once during my runs around the neighborhood or at the gym had my bones really affected my athletic ability. I prided myself on how strong I was even with all the exercising. A sharp sting rushed through my ankle. Damn it! How could this be happening? It only seemed like a minor roll, but the excruciating pain exploded.

Everything from Houston flashed in my eyes! I saw my aunt at the kitchen table telling me that it was my fault and then my uncle scolding me for going into that room. I remembered being in the exercise room with Mark's hands inside of me. I remembered the discomfort, the pure disgust, and the feeling of suffocating.

The varsity head coach called in the athletic trainer, who helped carry me to her office. Sniffling, I tried to breathe as the coach told me he was going to call my dad.

"Neesha, how are you feeling?" the coach asked.

"I'm fine. I just rolled it slightly," I said as my kneepad fell down, revealing my bony knee.

When my dad walked into the gym, he told the coaches he was taking me home. I could see his jaw clenching when he found me in the athletic training room. "I'm really sorry about this, coach."

"I hope she can make a quick recovery. The team really needs her. But her health is the most important thing. Just make sure she rests that ankle."

"I definitely will. Thanks again. Okay, let's go, Neesha," my dad said.

I knew this was more than a roll. My bones had never been this weak. "Dad, I just rolled it a little. I can still play," I said as we walked out of the gym.

"You're done, Neesha! You're done with volleyball. No more workouts or running, no more anything—you are *done*!"

"But Dad, it was just a roll."

"Just stop!"

So now volleyball was over. The one game that made me happy. The one thing I was good at. The game I loved was no longer in my life. As we headed to the car, my body felt heavier than usual. I lost the one thing that I had been looking forward to. The one thing that made me my old self.

I glanced at my iPod, trying to change the song to "Secret" by Maroon 5. I could barely see straight as we drove back home in silence. My dad seemed like he hated me, but I was furious with him for taking away the only passion I had left. I couldn't even look at him. We drove out of the school parking lot.

Staring out the window watching the desert road pass me by, I didn't even care how mad he was at me or why. We passed dirt roads heading up toward the Sandia Mountains. The town looked more desolate than usual during the day, when people were usually at work or school. There was always something comforting about the dry air in this town, something that made it home. It was a place I always wanted to come back to because growing up I associated it with being carefree. But now the heat felt heavy, and mountains no longer gave me the serenity of home.

My parents sat me down that afternoon at the kitchen table, giving me no choice but to face them. "Neesha, honey, we are seriously worried about you. You're so weak, and this has gotten out of hand. I don't even know what to say anymore," my mom said.

"This is ridiculous!"

"This is not okay, Neesha!" my dad shouted over me. "You're killing yourself. Do you understand that? You look tired. You have no energy. I'm relieved your ankle is okay, but you could have collapsed out there today! Do you know what could have happened, Neesha? Do you? Do you care?"

The lecture went in one ear and out the other as I focused on how to maintain the habits that now defined me. I held back my tears as much as I could. My mouth turned dry. I needed water so badly. But I just sat in the wooden chair as they stared at me. I was being prosecuted. I was on trial, and they needed answers. I was the defendant, and I was losing this case.

I was about to lose another.

23 ∘ *replay*
september, 2006

Once my sophomore year began, I felt like there was little to look forward to anymore. My emotions and body were numb. The mundane routine I submerged myself in had created an entirely different person. The notion of being the girl I was before now felt impossible.

Not long after the disastrous volleyball tryouts, I walked up the stairs at school and noticed how weak I was. I could barely make it up one flight. Was this was what I wanted?

I still wished to be a child again. To be innocent. To erase the memory. To make it all go away and start over. I wanted to be like everyone else again, but as badly as I hoped I could turn back time, I continued to lose the battle. The boys in Houston beat me. They won. They had everything, and I had nothing. As I walked up those stairs to go to my English class, I held on to the blue railings and tried to pull my body up. It felt like climbing Mount Everest.

I wasn't going to make it.

But then I thought of how satisfying it felt. I had a sense of power back in my life. I might have lacked endurance in my body, but why did it matter anymore if I couldn't play volleyball? My parents took that from me too, and I was left with only myself. The struggle to take back my life remained in the self-restriction I saw as strength. I was the king of my castle.

I was winning.

I was the only person I could trust, and I could go through life on my own.

My heart was completely separate from my body, and my body was split from my mind. I was at war with myself. Back and forth, like a volleyball over the net, choices in my head never stopped and thoughts never ended—whether it was what to eat, or what to look up on my computer, or how I could figure out a way to exercise without my parents knowing. The voice never went away.

I climbed up the stairs to my English class, but I just wanted to make it to the room and enjoy the class the way I used to. English had always been my favorite class. I never enjoyed math or science the way I loved English. If the books were interesting, I enjoyed the escape. That semester, our first book was *Play It as It Lays* by Joan Didion. Something about the ending struck me. I related to the protagonist, Maria, because of her lack of direction. I understood the feeling of not caring or not wanting to feel anything anymore but having to just keep going.

I looked forward to seeing Emma and Jane again, but the thought of seeing Brad after my birthday terrified me. We had not spoken since that day. I told Emma and Jane not to invite him to hang out with us anymore over the summer because of what happened. They probably thought I was insane, but I didn't care. When my parents asked why, I just told them he was busy. The thought of having a guy friend again just took me back to New Year's. I didn't need guy friends. In fact, I didn't really need any friends at all. I would be just fine on my own.

Back at home, everything continued to be routine. My family dinners were inescapable. I ate as little as possible but couldn't get away from my parents' watchful eyes.

"By the way, Neesha," my mom began one evening over dinner, "I'm picking you up from school tomorrow morning. The police want to record your account of the incident, for the case. So after your first class, I'll be there. Okay?"

What was I supposed to say? How was that a "by the way" comment?

Thoughts charged through my mind as we sat at the kitchen table. I was angry that I had no way to get out of the recording, and it didn't help my mood that my parents decided to serve chicken with mashed potatoes that night. With all the butter in the potatoes, I couldn't imagine how many calories it would be.

I hoped to cut as many foods out of my diet in order to eliminate stress, but it became yet another fight with my parents on why I couldn't eat this or that. Whether it was the amount of butter in the potatoes or too much dressing on the salad, I found an excuse for everything. I tried to calculate how many calories I would be eating for dinner, but my need for control would ruin my entire evening if I ate more than I planned.

As my parents stared at the television, I continued to stare at my plate. I ate six bites of my chicken and drank three glasses of water while I tried to ignore the calorie content. I thought if I could come around to spending time with my parents, maybe things could go back to how they used to be, but now I had to deal with this legal case again? Why? It had been months. As I thought about the next day, I became enraged and my head starting aching. I realized they still did not get it. Maybe I could tell them I had a test tomorrow or that I had a meeting with my English teacher. Or I could call Dr. Young and have her tell them we needed a last-minute appointment.

That would never work.

I couldn't use volleyball as an excuse anymore, but that was after school anyway. What if I said we could all go out for a family dinner and I would eat at whatever restaurant they wanted?

They would never believe that.

"Can I be excused?" I asked.

My mom looked at my plate and sighed. "You literally ate nothing. You need to finish your food. Why can't you just finish your dinner?"

"Mom, what do you want from me? I am here, and I am eating. You just said I have to go do a recording tomorrow! When do I get a say in anything I do? Is that ever going to happen?"

"Don't talk to your mom like that!" my dad interjected as he dropped his knife. Staring straight into his blue eyes, I could see his jaw clenching. I immediately looked away.

"Fine! Then just let me go to my room. I can't even think about this anymore. And I don't want to go tomorrow!"

"You have to go!" My mom attacked.

"No, I don't. I won't. I'm not going."

"Yes, you are!"

Back in my room, I looked in my mirror and saw that my hipbones weren't showing. My bloated stomach looked like a balloon from eating for the first time that day. But even though I feared how much weight I might have gained from the butter in the potatoes, I grew more terrified of what would happen with the recording. What were they going to ask me? Would they send the recording to my aunt and uncle? Would they send it to Will and Mark? Would they let my mom be in the room with me during the recording? Would my parents be able to watch it? Would it be played at a trial?

As questions dropped like bombs in my head one after the other, I began to remember everything about the exercise room. I recalled how the door closed and from that moment on I could not escape. I bit my lip the same way I did before Will forced himself in my mouth. I remembered him saying, "Just let me finish" when I wanted to leave. Why didn't I just leave? As I sat on my bed, I could even taste the putrid fluids in my mouth from that night. I thought about Will mouthing "Happy New Year" from across the room when the ball dropped on New Year's. I only remembered it as the last happy moment of being fourteen.

Anxious at 10:15 a.m., I left my English class. I walked to the car, struggling as the harsh wind acted like a barrier. I almost fell backward with every step I took. I tried once again to remember every detail of New Year's Eve so I could get my story straight before I had to discuss it. What time was it when everything happened? What was I wearing?

As I walked through my school's campus and began to remember Will's and Mark's faces, I saw their eyes, their bodies, and recalled how they made me feel. I remembered Mark's fingers being inside of me as my body went into shock. I couldn't imagine how he thought it was okay to do that to someone he knew for years, to someone he called a friend. I shuttered at the memories.

I passed red benches next to the cafeteria, stones lining the walkway next to the gym, and giant glass windows next to the main office. Arms folded across my chest, I shook my head and looked down as I tried not to think about the boys anymore. Passing all the cars of the administrators on the black asphalt, I saw my mom's silver Lexus. "Hi, honey," she said as I climbed into the car. "How are you?" she asked.

I responded with an exaggerated smile, no teeth showing.

As usual, the moment we pulled away, I plugged my ears with headphones and turned on "How to Be Dead" by Snow Patrol, one of my favorite songs. When we arrived at a police station, I realized I had never been there before; I'd only seen it in passing. The parking lot had two police cars in it, and they both had exhaust rushing out. I coughed as I stepped out of my mom's car noticing the garbage cans overflowing with trash. I shuffled into the massive brown building with stucco on the outside, lagging behind my mom. While she went to the front desk, I took a seat and waited for her, iPod still playing. No one else was sitting in the wooden chairs with worn-down red cushions. I didn't even want to touch the armrests, nervous about what disease I might pick up. The blue carpet was filled with dragged-in mud and dust from a lack of vacuuming. Living in some type of horror film, I never would have imagined this would be my fate.

Just let me go home. This place was worse than the rape clinic, I said to myself.

Shortly after we checked in, someone walked over and called out my name. I followed him down a narrow hall with beige walls and the same dirty carpet. So this was what it felt like to walk to a jail cell. It smelled like one too, or at least what I thought one might smell like. Musty, like unwashed clothes. I was a prisoner.

We arrived at a room with a square window on the door. Only

big enough for one person to see in and out of, it reminded me of a small window outside of an interrogation room. The man who led me there opened the dark gray door and motioned me inside, where the interviewer was waiting for me. He was a slightly overweight middle-aged Caucasian man wearing gray slacks, shiny black shoes, and a striped button-down shirt. He had dark brown hair and a dark brown bushy mustache. About six feet tall, he towered over me as he moved around searching for papers or pens. Unsure of what was about the happen, I held my breath until he sat down in his chair.

I wore my puffy white coat, jeans, and pink Uggs, the only outfit I felt remotely comfortable in. I heard the door shut and then the sound of a lock clicking. The moment I heard that click, it was official: I was trapped. Just like in the exercise room nine months ago, I was imprisoned. I was a mouse, and the interviewer was the cat that had his paw right on top of me. The same way Will did.

Two black chairs with matching cushions faced the camera with a small tan coffee table between them. Pens and three legal pads were stacked on top of the table. I took a seat. I was freezing. This must have been where murderers sit while getting interrogated. Sweating from nerves, I could feel my T-shirt becoming damp underneath my jacket.

The interviewer smiled. "Hello, Neesha. I'm John. How are you? Feel free to take off your coat."

No way, I thought. Not for you. Who did he think he was? I would never take off my jacket in this creepy room for this useless recording. Exposing myself at all to him would make this interview way too invasive. He pointed to the camera. "You don't have to look at it, but that's where it is."

Don't tell me what to do. "Thanks," I said.

"Of course, dear. It's right over there."

Did he really think I was that stupid? I heard him the first time. I hated being told what to do by this man. I had to get the hell out of here. How could I escape? I couldn't jump out the window. I couldn't run to the corner of the room and refuse to do the interview. After all, my mother was in the waiting room, and the last person I wanted to tell this story to was her. If I pissed him off enough, I was sure he would bring her in, and that would make everything worse.

I didn't trust this man nor did I want to be in this room alone with him. I hoped that maybe someone could see us as we were recording. I feared that something bad would happen. I tried to keep some distance between us. I scooted my chair as far away from his as I could. I was sixteen inches away. I needed to be farther, but no amount would be enough.

The look on his face and his dismissive voice said that he was bothered by my rude actions. "So just start telling the story in as much detail as you remember. Don't leave anything out. Every detail of that night is important, even how many times everything happened," he said. It was clear he did not want to be there.

Rage burned inside of my body. My breathing became heavier and heavier as I tried to speak, but I just dropped my head in my hands. I got up from my chair and walked to a corner of the room with my hands over my eyes and came back a few seconds later. I sat back down and kept my eyes closed for a moment as I tried to push away the memory. I couldn't. I wished I had a coffee to distract myself, or my iPod. I wanted to be at school or doing homework or even taking a test. I couldn't tell this story. I just couldn't do it again! I would even eat again to please my parents. Whatever they wanted I would do it. Just not this. I would have done anything not to be in this police station.

Staring at the ground, I thought to myself, Why would I tell a stranger what I couldn't even face in my own mind?

The interviewer handed me a legal pad. "If you can't say the words for certain things such as *penis* or anything else, just write them down or draw them—any terms you can't say out loud or don't feel comfortable with."

Penis. Was he serious? Like I would, in a million years, draw what happened that night. I couldn't think about those things. I couldn't think about a penis. I didn't want to think about Will's penis in my mouth. I didn't want to remember the night my entire life fell apart and destroyed everything. Wanting to strangle him and shove him off his seat, I considered spitting on him. He deserved it.

My face burned. An excruciating heat that needed to end. Overwhelming flashes of warmth shot through my body, and I gripped the armrests of my chair. Where do I start in the story of that night? What do I tell him? Do I say nothing happened and this is all made up? Do I say it was just Will and me in the room? Do I say this is my fault? Do I tell him I tried to leave every single second I was in that exercise room, but I could not find the strength to get up and go? Do I tell him how I knew Mark all those years yet he still did this to me? Do I tell him that I will never forget how scarring that experience was for the rest of my life? Do I tell him I want Will to go to jail for what happened that night? What was I even supposed to say? I didn't even know how to say it out loud anymore.

"Basically Will forced me to give him head."

And that was it.

The moment I spoke that last word, tears streamed down my face. I had used a teenage slang word; that made me a teenager. I wanted my innocence back. Too afraid to say anything else, I cried in my hands and took the tissue the interviewer handed to me.

"What do you mean when you say 'head'?" the interviewer asked.

Infuriated that he felt the need to turn this into a conversation, I glared at him—similar to the one I gave Mark when he hugged me New Year's morning. It was a hug of surrender. The moment when the battle is lost and there's nothing else to do but be compliant. So I tried my hardest to get through this interview.

With my dark brown eyes staring at the floor, I answered, "Oral sex."

With that, I gave him the exaggerated, fake smile a raging teenager gives her mom when she knows she is right. Eyebrows raised and everything. I wasn't the child I wished to be anyway, so I might as well show him how mature I was now. I shook my head as guilt over that night filled me. I now had more anger toward this interviewer than I ever imagined. Why did he need to know this story? He frivolously looked at his legal pad, disregarding the fact that there was a crying fifteen-year-old girl in the room. He needed sensitivity training. I didn't want to talk about this with him. Didn't he know that?

But I had no choice.

"Mark fingered me," I continued at a faint whisper.

"What do you mean? Can you tell me more about that?"

"I mean..."

"Like, can you define what that means so we are clear?"

"Um...no"

"Okay, how many times did he finger you?"

I guess I'm actually going to have to say something.

"About three times, I think."

"Was this during the time Will was making you give him oral sex?" he asked.

Finally realizing how disturbing that night was with two boys and me locked in that room, I looked at him with a sense of understanding—with more pain in my eyes than anyone my age should ever have. "Yes." I answered.

"How did he go about this?"

I had no desire to continue with the story.

"I don't know."

I was humiliated.

"Well, how many times did he force himself inside you? How did this happen?"

"Look...I don't even know."

The interviewer asked about all the grueling details regarding Will, but I just felt incredibly nauseous thinking about them. From what liquids were in my mouth to how many times Mark stuck his fingers inside of me. And how many fingers. Appalled that he would even need to know these intimate details disturbed me, and I couldn't believe he was so comfortable asking me.

I stopped crying at some point, just wanting to finish the story. He asked how the incident ended, and I told him that my aunt walked in. Will and I were the only ones in the room by that time, I explained. He asked when Mark had left, but I didn't remember.

Not a lie.

He asked for the specifics about what went in my mouth. Like I would use those words with him. I understood that this was a legal case, but I wanted to run out of that room and be by myself. Finally, looking away, I told him that Will never finished in my mouth.

I was completely mortified.

He would not stop asking questions. He asked for details about what Mark had done with me. He insisted he needed to know more details "about the assault."

I remembered the pressure of my knees on the rough, carpeted floor in the exercise room. I imagined how my body would have looked if someone had seen it, how my thighs shook violently that night. I remembered feeling paralyzed and how my body wouldn't let me get up and walk out of that room.

He asked more questions about the sexual acts, but I stopped responding. I couldn't bear to talk about it anymore and just thought about how many calories I ate so far today. I added a "yes" here and there when he asked me if it was dark or what doors were located where in the exercise room, but I had pretty much braved all I could. I mentioned a bit about what we were doing before any of this happened, where everyone was sleeping. He asked me everything the detective had asked me on the phone, but all I wished was for everyone to stop asking me about it.

Didn't anyone notice that this was not something I wanted to talk about, let alone on videotape?

Finally, the interviewer sighed after twenty minutes. "I have the basic story. Since you're really not giving us much to work with, that's about it. You can head out."

I wiped my tears one more time and handed him my unmarked legal pad.

"Thanks for your cooperation," he said with a firm nod. "Detective Reynolds will be following up and calling you soon."

I nodded my head and tried to force a fake smile, but nothing happened. He opened the door, and I shuffled out of the room as quickly as possible.

The interviewer followed me back to the waiting room. The florescent lighting blinded me, even with tears in my eyes. I hadn't noticed it before, but then I saw my mom sitting on the torn-up, cheap furniture as she stood and walked over to us. I sat down and let out a sigh, staring at the ground. I rubbed my eyes, trying to make them less red so my mom wouldn't think I was crying.

"How did it go?" my mom asked the interviewer.

"She was quiet, to say the least, but I think we have more information than we had before. She seems really shook up still—I hope she is okay."

"Yeah, she hasn't been taking any of this well at all," my mom said softly.

"Well, I wish you guys the best of luck."

"Thank you so much. We'll be in touch."

I took out my phone and thought about texting Emma or Jane but ended up staring at the blank screen instead. I had no desire to tell them that I had to repeat this story on tape. How can I block out this entire experience? That's what I had been trying to do for months. I tried consuming myself in the blogs. I listened to my iPod all the time. I tried to be the girl I used to be, and I now fit in my pink shirt. I tried to pretend like it never happened. I tried to change the way I looked to prevent it from happening again. I tried to play volleyball again to be with my friends. I drank coffee every morning like an adult. I tried to be an adult. I tried to be a kid. I tried everything.

Why wouldn't anyone let me put this in the past?

I glanced up as my mom shook the interviewer's hand, and I jumped up as fast as I could. So this was actually at a police station. Walking ahead of my mom to the car, I couldn't even turn to look back at her.

She took me to Starbucks on the way home because that was the only place I would go when she asked if I wanted to go out to lunch. No way did I want to eat at a restaurant.

"Please just give me a break. I'm really not hungry. That was the worst thing I've ever done. Please, please, can we not fight? I just want coffee and a nap."

"I'm sorry if that was awful, but Neesha, we're just trying to get to the bottom of this. We're all trying to help you."

This wasn't helping me at all. "Yeah, sure," I said.

She stopped the car at Starbucks and handed me a five-dollar bill. I walked in, thankful that the interview was over. I ordered a Grande black coffee. The barista gave me $2.12 back. I took the coffee and didn't even bother to put Splenda in it.

Walking back to the car, I slipped one of the dollars in my pocket and gave my mom $1.12 back.

"What did you get?" she asked.

"A vanilla latte."

We drove home as I drank my coffee and listened to my iPod. Did she know what she just put me through? I so badly wanted to scream at everyone for doing this to me, but I held in my anger. Beyond my anger for her and the interviewer, I was left with one question: where was the justice in this situation? If that was what my parents wanted, they were not getting it. This was just causing more pain. Not more pain for anyone in Houston—more pain for me. This didn't punish the boys. They were punishing me. Months and months had passed. What was the point of any of it anymore?

We arrived home, and I walked inside ahead of her, slamming the garage door behind me before she could even get out of the car. I bolted to my room and set down my coffee. I went to the mirror, looking directly into my eyes, red and gushing. I stared at myself with deep, passionate disgust. I started crying out loud now, no longer sweet, calm tears but aggressive sobs that stung my chest. I cried so hard that it burned my stomach and my lungs.

I needed to feel that pain.

My face stung as I touched it with my freezing hands. I looked at my face in the mirror again; it was drenched not only with salty tears, but with spit as well. I squeezed my stomach as hard as I could because I wanted more pain. I thought throwing up would evoke the suffering I needed to feel at this moment.

I wanted to bend my hand back far enough to cause something to tear in my wrist. I craved that throbbing stretch but worse. I wanted to open my mouth and pluck my teeth out one by one. I wanted to pull my hair out and feel so much more pain than I had felt when Will had run his hands through my hair that night. I wanted to scratch my face so badly that it didn't look like me. I didn't want to be me anymore.

24 ∘ *one, two, three*
october, 2006

Defeat overcame me. As bad as the phone calls had been with the detective, the police interview sent me straight back to that night. I was getting off the plane from Houston over and over and over again.

Having to the say the words *penis in my mouth* and even the word *finger* made my skin crawl. I felt like there were insects eating my body. I couldn't stand being in my skin. I wanted to burn it off. I needed to tear off each and every layer of my skin until only my bones were left. I did not want to live anymore.

One evening when I sat in my black chair alone in my room listening to music, one song ended and the next was about to begin, but in that split second of silence, I started to think about being under the blanket in that exercise room. And that was one moment I tried to avoid for months.

The most horrifying thought was that red blanket covering my head. Smothered and completely without air. My vision was blurred from the cloth in my face, and the tears in my eyes made it even harder to see. I thought about how Will's penis filled my mouth, how frightening it was not to breathe, and how painful it felt as my jaw was forced open.

Thinking about him made me want to destroy my fifteen-year-old body. I couldn't even stand to see myself. It was unbearable to look in the mirror at night. I lay on the floor curled in the fetal position, soft tears rolling down my cheeks. All of a sudden I felt more alone than ever.

That was the first time I had ever questioned who I really was.

My throat started hurting, just like it had in the exercise room. I tried to convince myself that it was all in my mind, but it felt so real again, like something was scratching the back of my throat.

I bit my lips like a baby refusing a spoonful of mashed carrots. The thought of anything in my mouth was enough to turn my stomach. Rolling side to side on my floor, I couldn't shake the anxiety.

I needed to do something to kill the pain I felt inside.

I needed to kill my insides.

Around 8:30 p.m., I finally found the strength to get up and walk to the hall bathroom. My parents had gone upstairs by now, without even saying good night. I opened drawers as fast as I could and slammed them shut. After looking through thin cardboard boxes of Tylenol or Nyquil, I finally found what I was looking for: Ex-Lax. I punched the little white pills out one at a time.

One.

Two.

Three.

I took all three laxatives at once. I turned on the silver faucet and bent my head over to wash down the pills. I had never been able to swallow pills as a child, so when I washed them down with water, I felt a sharp pain. But for the first time, it was rewarding. I sighed and felt powerful knowing I could get rid of what was inside me with such ease.

Oblivious to how dangerous this was with only a sandwich and maybe two sections of an orange in my stomach from that whole day, I waited. I strolled back to my room with a little hop in my walk, as if I'd won a contest. I jumped on my bed and let out a sigh. I picked up my phone to text Emma about the district championship volleyball game happening that night. I sent her a "good luck" text since my mood had improved. She had taken my spot on varsity, but I pretended like I didn't care.

I then rolled from the bed to the floor and pulled out my laptop to browse the blogs. I checked a few gossip websites for fun and looked at a volleyball site that had the statistics of my high school games, but after a few minutes they just reminded me of how much I wanted to be playing again. I opened up my backpack and looked at the homework that was due the following week. Beginning the reading for Chemistry, I made it through two of the six assigned chapters. I read them over and over to make sure I understood what was going on, but then I finally looked up at the time. Two hours had passed, and I realized I forgot everything I just read.

My stomach began to grumble—not the usual noises of hunger but something more distressed. I reclined on the floor with a groan as my belly expanded like a balloon being blown up at rapid speed. Cramps made my insides turn, the kind of cramps that made my abdominals painfully weak. It felt like my organs were being plucked with tweezers or like a surgeon was examining my insides, but I could feel the procedure. I glanced at the clock again as I felt a sting with an impulse to go back to the bathroom. It was 10:30 p.m.

I rushed to the bathroom, the fastest fifteen steps I had taken in months.

I slammed the door behind me and turned on the two lights next to the toilet, one a heat lamp and one a regular light. I dropped my black sweatpants down my legs and sat on the toilet. A clear liquid flowed out of my body, but my belly was so swollen it looked like a baby was inside.

The bathroom spun at a thousand miles per hour.

I fell off the toilet to the right. Desperately trying to pull up my pants, I grabbed at my legs as they shook violently. I had never shaken like this before. Feeling like my body had a mind of its own, I kept shaking as I desperately gasped for air.

I lay on the furry pink bath mat in my bathroom and held my stomach. I tried to slow my breathing but continued to pant faster than a track runner, my lungs pounding. With my eyes shut, I could only think about the excruciating pain in my stomach.

I heard an urgent rush of liquid in my belly. Frantically, I crawled back onto the toilet. Eyes closed once more, I emptied my watery bowels.

But my arm muscles could not hold my head and shoulders up any longer. My legs bounced up and down four times per second as I placed my hands on my knees. Pushing down on my legs, I hoped to get everything out of my body—the laxatives, the food, the pain of everyone in my life, and especially my family in Houston who I never wanted to hear from again.

But the pain remained.

I fell to the floor once again. This time, I could not open my eyes.

I tried to get back onto the toilet, pushing as hard as I could against the floor. But I fell to the ground again and lay there trembling. This continued for hours, briefly passing out until the pain subsided enough for me to open my eyes. At one point I was able to look at the clock. It read 1:30 a.m. I thought about how incredible sleep would feel right now, but I could not lift my body up enough to get into the bedroom.

I finally forced myself up to stand. I fell over the sink and tipped my head to drink a sip of water. My throat felt like I just finished a run in the summer heat. I needed water. I looked in the mirror at my eyes, but I couldn't see straight. The mirror was spinning me around and around. What I could see in it made me want to punch the mirror. I saw the outline of my body, my legs that would not stand still, and my ballooned stomach.

Then the pressure in my inflated stomach struck me. I sat down on the toilet again, resting my elbows on my knees now. They bounced up and down, like a child on his grandpa's lap. My eyes burned as I pressed my hands against them as hard as possible. Once my body let out a rush of what felt like water, I felt my stomach drastically shrink. Letting out a deep sigh, I looked at the clock to see that it was now 3:00 a.m.

I wiped and looked at the toilet paper. It was dark red.

Blood. Thin, runny blood.

With wide eyes, I forced myself to look at the toilet. A mixture of yellow and clear liquids swam in the toilet water. But a layer of crimson blood covered the mixture.

I flushed the toilet and watched the liquids disappear.

The sight of blood revolted me. I had been afraid of it since I could remember. Seeing the red liquid in my toilet worried me. I was already winning the battle of having no period; I was the child I wanted to be, at least physically. But now my thoughts spiraled out of control. I couldn't think straight, imagining my parents talking to me, hearing Emma's voice speaking to me, hearing a phone ringing.

My dysfunctional mind convinced my body that it was itchy. I began scratching my legs out of desperation. Convinced that quiet knocks were tapping on the door despite the hour, I cried, "One second!" But I didn't get a response. Lying on my pink bath mat, a rush of fear struck me. I couldn't look at the mirror because I thought someone would be in it. Convinced that people, thieves, police officers, or anyone else were standing behind my mirror, looking right at me, I just shook.

Completely frantic.

The fear only lasted about fifteen minutes as I lay on the mat.

My body felt like it had no liquid in it anymore. Once I felt conscious enough to stand up, I forced myself to drink as much water as I could. I fell back onto the bath mat, waiting until I had to pee. Sure enough, I jumped back up with urgency. Once on the toilet, I had to wait ten seconds before my body would let me urinate.

It burned. The only other time it had hurt me to pee was after New Year's Eve. But the pain just reminded me of all the agony I had endured over the past ten months.

I pulled up my pants and stood. Dehydrated and empty, I struggled back to my room and lay on the side of my bed. Now 4:00 a.m. with closed eyes, my mind raced back and forth between the police interview and how I had missed the biggest volleyball game of the season. I didn't even go support Emma. I was too concerned with myself. Too consumed with killing my insides.

25 ∘ *no thanks*
october-november, 2006

Avoiding volleyball and avoiding friends, I continued to immerse myself in solitude. Selfish and isolated, I brushed by Jane and Emma in the lunchroom for the rest of October, avoiding them and any possible conversation. My mood, down and cold, kept me from talking to my only two friends. I felt ashamed and embarrassed when I would see Emma with her carefree life. She had it all, and I began to resent that she was a star on the volleyball team and that everything came easily to her.

Nothing came easily for me anymore. One day I heard them in the library and knew they were concerned.

"Where has Neesha been? The coaches were asking me about her in practice yesterday, but I didn't know what to say," Emma told Jane.

"I know. I feel so bad. I wish she would just get help or, like, talk to us. I don't know what else to do, and she is completely ignoring Brad. What is going on with them?" Jane asked.

"I mean, she's still so upset about what happened at her birthday, but he doesn't even know what to do. He feels so bad. I was talking to him about her last night."

They didn't know I was in the library that day during our free period, and I made sure they didn't see me. Feeling hurt and betrayed,

I couldn't realize that they just wanted to see me happy again and be their friend again. I passed Brad in the hall that day at school, but I looked down. He texted me every few days to see if there was something he could do, but there really wasn't. It broke my heart that I couldn't trust him anymore because joy was now out of my life. No one else could make me laugh that way.

Now, every time I went home in the car with my dad, I just kept quiet. In the mornings my mom would make me a breakfast burrito to take to school, and I would muster up a "thanks" but ended up tossing it once I went to my first class. There was no point in arguing with them anymore. I'd sprint straight into the living room and watch television while my mom tried to talk to me about my day. I still resented her for forcing me to do the interview.

When Halloween came, I tried to remember the year before, when we all went trick or treating together in Brad's neighborhood. We ended up bringing rolls of toilet paper and TPing houses instead of getting candy. Feeling like rebels for a night, we all broke the rules for the first and last time together.

One afternoon after art class, Emma and Jane approached me with looks of concern.

"Hey, we know you haven't been around a lot, but we were thinking we could still spend Halloween together. Last year was so fun, and Brad really wants to see you too. We think you should give him a chance. I mean, come on. You guys have been best friends for years. You need to let this go because we all can tell you miss him," Emma said.

Best friends? Since when can I trust best friends? I thought Mark used to be one of those so-called best friends of mine. Look how that turned out.

"I know. I do. It's just that now is really not a good time."

"Neesha, what is going on? We miss you so much, and you have been avoiding us all semester. Please, will you come hang out with us tonight?" Jane asked.

"I miss you guys too. I have a lot to deal with right now and want to come, but I don't know if I can. You guys don't understand what I'm dealing with."

"Understand what? Please let us in. You can tell us anything," Jane said.

I began to shake. "It's everything from New Year's. I can't let go of what happened. I'm miserable. I can't even tell you how bad I'm feeling. I have to see this fucking shrink who I hate. My parents don't get that I want this to go away. They don't get that I need to completely forget about it so I can move on. I hate my family in Houston and don't even care if I ever talk to them again and…everything is falling apart, and I don't know what to do."

"But Neesha, you know we are here for you. You must be having a really hard time. I'm so sorry you have to go to therapy," Emma said as she tried to give me a hug.

"Thanks. Yeah, my therapist is awful. She just keeps interrogating me every time I go in there, and I'm so upset about not being able to play volleyball."

"I am sure you are, and I am so sorry that they made you stop playing. It's totally unfair. We all miss you so much," Emma said.

"Thanks. I appreciate it guys. But I don't even know what to do anymore. I'm so over this. All of this. I keep trying to keep it together, but then something happens to make me miserable."

"I'm sorry, Neesha. I wish you would let us be here for you. We need to see each other more. You should come to some of the soccer games with Emma," Jane suggested.

"I do miss them. I literally feel trapped, for so many reasons that you probably don't even understand. And my parents don't trust me at all anymore. Like, at all."

"You just need to talk to them. I'm sure if you guys talk about it, you can figure all this stuff out," Jane said.

Like I would do that. "I know. I might try sometime."

"So will you come hang out with us on Halloween?" Emma asked.

"I don't know. I'm not sure if my parents will let me. Can I let you know after school?"

"Yeah, sure. And really, if you need anything at all, we're here for you," Emma said with a smile.

On the drive home, my dad asked me if I wanted to hang out with my friends. He said he was willing to drive me to see Emma and Jane. I told him, "No, it's okay. I don't think they are doing anything tonight. Everyone has a lot of homework."

"Oh, okay," he said.

I took out my phone to text Emma and wrote, *Hey, my dad said we have to have dinner tonight and I don't think he wants to drive me after it. I'm sorry. Can you tell Jane for me?* My plans then consisted of watching TV when I got home after briskly walking to the living room as I shouted a "hello" to my mom. My parents ordered pizza for dinner, and I managed to convince them to let me eat my slice in my room. The truth was my parents couldn't win one way or another. If they made me eat at the table, I would start an argument, and if I left, I would flush most of my dinner down the toilet.

I was winning. I was in control.

I would never eat pizza now, but I missed the days when I never thought about calories. I used to dunk a slice of pizza into ranch dressing every movie night with my friends. And then go back for seconds.

I slammed the door shut behind me, setting my plate down with the slice of pizza and went about my usual workout routine. I had started stretching and doing leg lifts on the bedroom floor now that running wasn't an option. Changing out of my jeans into my black sweatpants and pink sweatshirt, I didn't even bother looking at the mirror. I knew I looked exhausted and disgusting, so I just started my routine by trying to touch my toes. The feeling of my hamstrings about to snap comforted me; it was the pain I deserved since I couldn't exercise at the gym. I took a little break to take a bite or two of pizza, which I chewed twenty times each before swallowing. Then I broke the rest of the pizza into little pieces, licked my fingers, sneaked into the bathroom, and then flushed the pieces down the toilet.

After heading back to my room, I finished my forty-five minute workout. My goal for sit-ups was two hundred per night, and

Halloween was no exception. I did my workout to an upbeat playlist that motivated me, giving me a break from the sullen songs I favored.

After my workout, I did exactly what I had told myself I would do on Halloween night: spend the night by myself watching TV. The holiday ended with an emptiness that comforted me. I no longer knew how to be anything but vacant.

But I also became even more volatile than before. With immense resentment toward my parents, I didn't even want to look at them, and I never took Jane's advice about talking to them. I began to talk back to them when they spoke to me, paranoid that their comments were insults or attacks. Since they still would not allow me to run after school, I hated them even more. I lived in a box where no one could get to me, and I convinced myself that my unhappiness was their fault.

Soon Thanksgiving was only a couple of days away, and my anxiety heightened. Spending my nights plotting how I would get through Thanksgiving dinner, I searched for the calorie content of foods that would be at the table. I stayed up in my room and held my breath before I hit "enter" on the calories of stuffing or the gravy I might have to eat. Blood boiling and my heart racing, I couldn't even think about those foods drenched in butter and salt.

Once the holiday finally arrived, I wore baggy jeans and a black sweatshirt. This was the first time that we celebrated Thanksgiving without my uncle and aunt in Houston, and I could tell it was on everyone's mind, especially my mom's. Earlier I heard my parents discussing the case, catching comments from my room like "I talked to our lawyer today" and "The detective should call tomorrow," but I pleaded they would not bring up the topic at dinner.

Just try to remain calm. You don't have to eat everything they put in front of you. Try to only eat half of it. Have a sip of water between each bite. Keep the conversation to small talk. Only light conversation, I told myself as I paced back and forth in my room.

During Thanksgiving dinner, I didn't speak, and I ate very little. I knew my parents wanted to fix me, but no family dinner could do that. I pushed my food around my plate and cut my piece of turkey into eight pieces, each about the size of half a dime. I ate seven of them and didn't even bother putting stuffing on my plate. I put three giant spoonfuls of peas on my plate and focused on eating those. Insisting that I wasn't hungry, I had a sip of water between each bite to keep me full.

"No bread for me," I told my dad when he offered me the basket.

He shook his head and looked at my mom. They both had that look on their faces—the look of disappointment.

My dad's teeth clenched with fury. "You need to eat more than that!" he yelled at me. "Why are you starving yourself? You ate two bites of food! It's Thanksgiving. You're making this so miserable!"

On the defensive, I screamed back, "I'm not hungry!"

"You're never hungry! You don't eat anything! Eat something—you're killing yourself!"

"I'm going to that damn therapist like you told me," I argued. I had never used a curse word to my dad in my life, but now I didn't care. "I don't run after school. I don't exercise at all. But all you two are doing is trying to fatten me up. I am not going to eat your fattening food and gain weight just because you say to! I just won't!"

"Neesha, you're acting like such a child. What the hell is wrong with you? Are you ever going to grow up? Ever?" my dad asked.

You don't think what I've gone through is grown up enough? "Nope. Never," I muttered under my breath.

"Neesha, you're ruining this family. You can't do this to your mom or me. I don't know what to do with you anymore. I really don't. We've tried everything, and all you do is act like this."

I slammed the silver fork on the glass plate, stood up, and walked to my room. They didn't even bother yelling at me.

I sure showed them.

I stomped out of the dining room and down the hall. I pounded my feet on the white tile floor, trying to make a point, but it only hurt my bones.

Done with dinner and done with my parents, I thought they might get it as I slammed my door shut. I wanted nothing to do with them.

They were the ones blowing this out of proportion—they caused this legal case. Maybe they were trying to punish Will and Mark, but they were punishing only me.

Infuriated, I thought about the interviewer's words: "If you can't say the words for certain things such as *penis* or anything else, just write them down or draw them. Any terms you can't say out loud or don't feel comfortable with." I remembered in disgust the words I'd had to say out loud: "Basically, Will forced me to give him head."

That still killed me. I never had so much trouble letting something go. Even a sentence I had to say. I couldn't just erase it from my brain. The words continued to repeat in my mind.

"Will forced me to give him head."

"Will forced me to give him head."

"Will forced me to give him head."

"Will forced me to give him head."

"Will forced me to give him head."

I wished there were a button to turn life off. I wanted to press "delete" on my laptop and have the past eleven months disappear. But there was no delete button. My childhood was gone, and there was no way to fix it.

Replaying the story again and again that I told on camera, I closed my eyes as tight as I could. Then suddenly, in my mind, all I could see was black. Not the boys' faces, not the blanket, not the camera—I just saw black. Breathing cautiously, with my eyes still closed, I saw black and nothing else.

I was terrified.

Rather than opening my eyes to see again, I squeezed them shut even harder, wanting to feel the pain in my eye sockets and cheekbones. A burning rushed up my nose, as if I'd just snorted some sort of drug. Rocking back and forth, I finally caught my breath, then I found the strength to open my eyes. No more blackness, just my room. The one for a child that didn't even feel like mine anymore. With a sigh, I climbed into my bed and fell into an irritated, stressful sleep.

November ended, and I no longer cared about anything. Or about anyone. Back to my secluded life, I remained exhausted. Back into my dark hole, where I fought to be a child. Alone. I felt like I had lost any sense of sanity in my life and was losing what little control I still had. I couldn't run when I wanted or not eat what I wanted. I felt very little toward my parents other than frustration and irritation.

I had given up.

My parents still forced me to go to my weekly visits on Mondays to Dr. Young, but I gave up on the kicking and screaming fits to get out of them. I went and stared at the floor answering her questions or sitting there in complete silence as I had done so many times before.

One Monday in December, I glanced down at my hands while sinking into the gigantic couch. My red nail polish had chipped on my pointer finger, and I could see the yellow nail beneath it. Doing a double take and trying to hide my finger, I couldn't stop staring at that chipped spot. I wore red nail polish constantly to hide my brittle nails, but with the polish chipped, I could see this wasn't normal.

Eventually I began actually talking to Dr. Young because I didn't think I had anything left to lose. In fact, I talked more in these sessions then I would in an entire week with my parents. Sometimes we would talk about real issues or absolutely nothing. I told her that it bothered me that my parents forced me to have dinner with them every night because I wasn't able to eat the foods I wanted. She asked me what foods I wanted to eat, and I made a big fuss about meat. "I feel horrible killing animals," I told her. "It's inhumane, and it frustrates me when my parents eat them. I don't want to kill animals."

Lie.

I started to use these sessions as a venue to rant since she had told me upfront that she never intended to make me gain weight. I told her that I missed volleyball and that my parents and I didn't really talk as much as we used to. I usually stayed in my room or watched TV most days.

She asked, "What do you usually do in your room when you're alone?"

"I talk on the phone with my friends or text or sometimes I read."

Because these meetings were only forty-five minutes, if I was in a bad mood, I would ramble about anything trivial. From the weather to clothes. I wanted to escape my true feelings, but I never showed her one bit of emotion, not even when I was talking about my parents or my frustrations. I never cried in front of her. I only cried alone.

I began to put on a happy face, even though I was not a pound heavier than when she first met me. I hoped she'd tell my parents I didn't need to see her anymore since I was finally speaking to her. But she didn't.

The one thing that did get under my skin was that she had meetings with my parents without me. She reiterated constantly, whenever I would bring them up, that everything in our sessions was confidential. But even so, I would always begin our conversations by asking, "You aren't going to tell my parents I told you this, right?"

This question would kill about ten of the forty-five minutes, because it would lead to her explaining the agreement to me.

Dr. Young tried to get me to plan sleepovers with Emma and Jane. She was trying to get me back on track, and I told her we saw one another all the time.

Lie.

I rarely talked to them.

She asked me how I felt about not speaking to my family in Houston anymore, and I told her I no longer cared about them. I needed to block them out. Forget about them. I said I needed to completely move on from them being in my life because I hated them. I wanted no contact, which was the truth. I never needed to speak to them again, and the happy memories of them no longer mattered to me. I had let it go. I really had. Hatred for them overwhelmed me, and I no longer needed to be emotional about it. I spent enough time being sad about them.

But Dr. Young had to have known that I lied my way through those sessions, especially when I talked about food. I found it amusing, another game; she was just a little therapist I played with. She thought she was so clever fixing me, but she wasn't.

It was one expensive game that my parents were paying for. And we weren't getting anywhere—we all knew that. I told her that food wasn't my issue and that nothing was wrong at this point except for the issues with my parents forcing me to eat things I didn't want. I placed the blame on them. All of the blame.

I sat on the brown couch each week, freezing, but I never mentioned to her that her office felt like an icebox. I actually felt more accomplished because I knew I burned more calories shivering on that couch. By now I wore sweatpants every week to her office to hide my tiny body from her probing eyes.

She chastised me about grades and mentioned that my parents talked a lot about my poor performance at school. I told her that I was doing better this year, and it wasn't anything to worry about. I rambled on about how last semester was a bigger challenge than this one and I was studying a lot more. Going to the library more. It wasn't a big deal.

I made it through the questioning by rambling on and making up excuses for my flaws.

I don't think she believed it. Any of it.

26 ∘ *last straw*
november, 2006

My mind was split between wanting to change my ways and sticking to my habits, but the latter seemed the easiest. I had fallen down a rabbit hole I could no longer climb out of. What I now saw in the mirror was not what everyone else saw. I knew the reflection was sick and frail, but I still gained satisfaction in denying myself food.

My weight determined how I acted that day. The feeling of being happy or sad when I saw the number on the scale felt impossible to break. Some mornings I tried not to weigh myself, but I always gave into the impulse. I had to know what the scale would say. But I had no direction. I could not find a way out. I felt like I needed to be numb, to feel nothing, to be nothing.

I began seeing loose strands of hair in my hairbrush the morning before the daily weigh-ins. Now there were a few more strands than usual. I started wearing winter hats to cover up my thinning hair, and then I avoided brushing it altogether due to the fear it gave me. I began taking hot showers twice a day to warm myself up, but when I would shampoo my hair and pull my hand out, a bundle of my long, black hair would appear.

Though shampooing scared me, showering actually made me less hungry. I would stay in the shower for an hour or more, usually shutting my eyes as a way to escape. I had read in the blogs that taking cold showers burned more calories, but I could never manage that. I showered with warm water because the second I stepped out, I shivered and trembled, my lips turning blue and white.

I longed for the years when winter and Christmas used to be my favorite time of year. Setting up the Christmas tree and putting on the ornaments with my mom was always a special tradition. The previous winter, I weighed 90 pounds, ate anything I wanted, hung out with the volleyball team, and had crushes on boys. Now, almost ten pounds lighter, I looked sick, I hated my parents, and I barely had friends.

My face revealed the fact that I couldn't sleep anymore. I bruised easily, and I had dark brown circles under my eyes. Whenever my parents told me that I looked tired, I blew them off by saying that I hadn't slept well. They noticed my sunken-in eyes and would mention them, but I told them that I was working on my sleep issues with Dr. Young.

"We're coming up with solutions for my sleep. I've never been a good sleeper," I would tell my mom. Little did she know that I continued to spend my nights tossing and turning in my bed, living in a memory that still haunted me.

Ever since the police interview, the nights had become the hardest. I went to sleep thinking about the two boys. Every night I would keep the lights on in my room and stay up until 2:30 a.m. I thought about what would have happened if I just stayed in Anita's room that night. Would my parents still be talking to my aunt and uncle? Would my family be normal again? Would Will and I be dating since he seemed to really like me? Or would Brad and I possibly be dating now? Would I have been on the varsity volleyball team and won the championship game with Emma next to me on the court? Would I still have my period? Would I still have a great relationship with my mom and dad? All these questions seemed worthless knowing the outcome I now faced. I could not even bear to be alone at night, but what choice did I have? I couldn't just erase the past year.

I was petrified to walk to the bathroom without a light on, scared of what might be around the corner. I jumped at the faintest noise. Shadows became real people in my mind. Howls of coyotes in the mesa came alive in my nightmares. I was a prisoner in my own house.

But more than that, I was prisoner of my past.

Since I had pushed my parents away, there was no point in even trying to open up to fix the problems. As a kid I never spent too much time holding grudges, but I couldn't understand how I was just supposed to forgive my parents. After all, I still had not forgiven myself for giving my parents any reason to take legal action at all.

Our relationship only frustrated me. Everything turned into a mundane series of arguments, but no one was willing to address the deeper issue. Through my anger and hatred, I still felt sympathy for my parents, who had no idea how to handle the situation. They were doing all they could to try and help, but I didn't know how to help myself. They had no way of knowing how to fix me. It was clear to everyone that I was broken.

There were no Christmas carols or cookies baking that December, just my mom warning me there would be one last call from the detective. Not the present I was wishing for. I was sick of adults still trying to tell me what to do and trying to get me to repeat the story. I had no trust in any of them. My parents, the detective, the police interviewer, my therapist—all of them. Would it ever end?

The detective called my house halfway through December. My mom answered, "Hi, yes, we've been waiting for your call. I've been well, and yourself?" She then walked over to me and handed me the phone.

"Hello, Neesha," he said.

How many times are we going to do this? "Hi," I said with a sigh.

"Here's where we're at: I've talked to the two boys, Anita, Rob, Lisa and Kate, and your aunt and uncle."

My heart raced. "Okay."

"The fact is that this will turn into a he-said/she-said case with you pitted against everyone else. Mainly the two boys. Your aunt and uncle said they heard you go into the exercise room that night and they believe Will and Mark. The boys said that you flirted with Will all night. Basically, you will have to go to court, possibly multiple times, in order to get the boys prosecuted."

Acid from my stomach shot up my throat as I coughed.

"Now Neesha, I need more from you," the detective went on. "I need you to make a real stand and show me some willpower—I need you to show me that you want to fight the case. The video didn't make a big enough impact as evidence, not enough for the boys to be prosecuted. And the clothes you gave us had insufficient evidence on them to prove what happened."

I wanted to hang up the phone and throw my shoe through the window I was looking at. I wanted to go into my kitchen and break every plate, bowl, and glass in the cupboards. I wanted to get a hammer and bust every television, mirror, and glass door in my house. I wanted to rip every piece of clothing, every blanket and sheet in my house, and burn it all down. I wanted everyone involved in this case to go to hell.

Why was this still part of my life?

I wanted nothing to do with my family in Houston—especially Will and Mark. I couldn't comprehend that my aunt and uncle believed that this was my fault. My blood boiled, and my muscles tensed. They felt so restless that I could barely breathe, and I had to blink three times to even remember that this wasn't a dream. Gasping with the phone cradled against my ear, I bit my nails without saying a word. The detective, silent now, had nothing left to say.

Finally as I ripped off part of my skin making my finger bleed, I blurted out, "Okay. Well honestly I won't do that. I refuse to do that. I can't."

I hung up the phone, hoping that I was hanging up on that night forever.

Assuming my parents already knew the verdict, I didn't bother taking the phone to my mom or telling her what the detective said.

In only my pink tank top and black sweatpants, my body was drenched in sweat as I lay on the white carpet of my bedroom floor.

When I looked at my shirt, I saw liquid dripping down the sides. Glistening moisture collected on my arms, and I thought my body temperature must have hit a hundred degrees.

I had been freezing for months, and all of a sudden I was sweating.

I ran to the bathroom. I thought I needed to throw up. With my face in the toilet bowl, I retched three times, but nothing came up. I wiped away a few tears that had fallen during my coughing. Back in my room, I lay down on my bed and climbed under the two comforters even though I was still sweating.

Heat rushed through my body. My face, buried in the pillow, was soaked along with my bangs. They fell back into my eyes immediately after I pushed them away—salty moisture mixed with newly fallen tears. Closing my eyes, I tried to fall asleep, but the flashbacks streamed through my mind.

I thought about the call I had with the detective, but it never registered that the two boys needed to be punished for what they did. For the first time, I regretted being so resistant to participating in the legal case. Instead of blaming my parents for forcing it on me, we should have fought as a family. I wished I had the courage to stand up for myself. To stand up for the truth. After all, I was taking the punishment for the boys. I was killing myself for both of them. I had finally realized…

I did nothing wrong.

27 ∘ *hunger hurts*
december, 2006

Winter break of sophomore year had finally arrived, and I felt like I could try to relax without school. Surprisingly I managed to get my GPA up to a 3.0 thanks to my A in English, which got my parents off my back. Since it was winter break, my parents didn't force me to eat dinner with them. They actually let me go on my walks outside since I received the grades they wanted. They knew I was miserable.

"Don't you want to see Jane and Emma?" my mom asked.

"I really am trying to focus on myself this break. I'm hoping to get some reading done. Dad just bought me a new book by Joan Didion that I want to read."

"Okay, well I guess that's good," she answered.

One Monday afternoon as I strolled down the park road, I passed a runner from a different private school in town. She held herself up with strength as she took long strides. I felt a pang of sadness as I listened to Snow Patrol, only this time it was because I realized I didn't want to be on this walk. I wanted to be with my friends. I wanted to be warm again and laugh again and have strength to go on a run like that girl was doing.

For the first time it hit me that the counting of calories was making me even unhappier. My bones hurt constantly. I was so thin that when

I would lie on my floor it hurt my spine. I didn't want to be in constant pain anymore. I was so used to it by now, but seeing someone pass by me on the park road made me feel weak. I couldn't keep up with that girl if I tried. I used to be one of the best athletes on the volleyball team, and now I wasn't even on the team. What was left to accomplish on my walks? Burning more calories? For what? Just so I could go back and watch television? This realization hit me hard and offered no solutions. I still had not found the inner strength to let go of the past.

I tried every trick to curb my hunger, but it was never enough. I stopped looking in my full-length mirror to see if my bones were visible. I knew they were. I looked so ill that I didn't even want to see my face. I was ashamed of myself.

After I would go to the bathroom, I would wash my hands as fast as possible, staring at the white sink to avoid the mirror. Seeing myself reminded me of my loneliness. I wished so desperately to be that pretty girl that Brad couldn't stop complimenting, but I knew he wasn't going to be in my life anymore. Jane and Emma had given up trying to contact me over the break because I told them I was busy. I ignored texts from both of them. I really didn't want to put in the effort, and I needed to focus on maintaining my weight. It was the only thing that I put energy into anymore. My mind would not let me think about anything else.

I lived in a nightmare where I was constantly drowning. I flailed in the ocean with the waves pulling me under the tide and I could not keep my balance. Taking deep breaths right before the waves hit, I failed to find the power to lift myself up. I tried to grab anything that would save me. I searched for someone's hand, but no one was there. Gasping and coughing, I hunted for that person to pull me out of the water.

But even if that hand existed, I don't think I would have grabbed it.

The winter nights were the most painful because they directly reminded me of how I had felt the year before. I remembered how excited I was to visit my family in Houston all by myself. Like an adult. I was going to have the best New Year's of my life! All grown up with my older cousins and the older boys. We were going to toast, and maybe I would even get to drink my first glass of champagne. We would stay up all night, and who knew—maybe I would get kissed at midnight. It would be the biggest moment ever if a boy kissed me. I had never been kissed before. Would it happen in Houston? Maybe I could come back and tell Jane and Emma that an older boy liked me or one of Rob's friends said I was cute. Maybe I would have a fairy-tale New Year's and something exciting would happen. Anything. It didn't even have to be a kiss, just something magical.

On the Thursday before Christmas, I went through my usual routine of going on a walk in the morning, and then I took a nap during lunchtime. My mom and I were supposed to put up the ornaments on the Christmas tree together, but I ended up doing it alone, placing each one perfectly on the tree while I watched *A Christmas Story* on TV in the living room. My parents were a room away watching the same movie.

"Neesha, dinner is in an hour!" she called to me over the television. "I'm making you salmon. I expect you to sit down with us tonight. You ate in your room last night."

I had told my parents that fish was the only meal I was willing to eat anymore.

"Okay, fine," I shouted back.

I could smell the raw fish from the living room. Despite what I said to my parents, I hated fish. I walked into the kitchen to find a giant piece of salmon waiting to be cooked, a portion much bigger than what I would ever eat.

"Is this for everyone?" I asked.

"No," she answered. "Dad and I are having steak."

I briskly walked back to my room and did a little bit of stretching and two hundred sit-ups to prepare for the fish I would be eating in an hour.

I couldn't bear to think of the calories. I brought my laptop down to the floor after the sit-ups and searched for the calories in a four-once fillet of salmon. Were there really 234 calories in it? I panicked but knew that it could be a lot worse. As long as I scraped off the skin and any sort of liquid that touched the fish, I would be fine. When I glanced down the screen a little bit, my panic doubled: 14.1 grams of fat!

My jaw dropped.

Restless now, I paced back and forth in my room. I tried to figure out how I would deal with eating this piece of fish. I opened up my laptop and researched laxatives. 14.1 grams of fat just couldn't stay in my body. I then searched for how much time it would take my body to absorb the fat.

What was I going to do? I couldn't say I had homework. I couldn't tell them I was going to Jane's or Emma's house for dinner. There was only an hour before we had to eat. They wouldn't let me eat in my room, so maybe I could eat in the living room? That wouldn't work. I could eat really fast then run to the bathroom and throw up. No way, I could never do that again after my birthday. I had never felt so disgusting. There was no way out. I was going to have to eat the salmon, but maybe I could still get rid of it.

I researched the laxatives again. I read on one website that a doctor had seen patients who abused ten laxatives a day. He also saw patients who abused up to two hundred laxatives a day. Eyes wide, I grew hesitant about the whole thing and decided I would see how I felt after dinner. If I felt like I could manage to keep the food in my stomach, I would try to do four hundred more sit-ups and some leg lifts to work it off.

A quick, loud knock on my door startled me out of my thoughts. I clicked out of the window and screamed, "Coming!"

"Dinnertime," my mom replied.

Shuffling down the hall in my usual attire, I walked into the kitchen and saw the salmon once again. I looked to the right of the fish and saw what I dreaded most: mashed potatoes. I sighed angrily.

I looked at my mom as I sat down at the table. "I don't want any potatoes."

My dad glared at me. "You're only eating a piece of fish? You can eat some potatoes. There's nothing wrong with potatoes. You need more than fish."

I put half a spoonful of potatoes on my plate.

"That's it? Half a spoonful! Look, we've let this go on long enough. You need to knock it off!"

"What are you talking about?"

"I mean with all this damn eating stuff. You got what you wanted—the legal case is over—so can't we all just move on?"

Move on? I have been trying to turn back and be who I was before any of this happened. "Are you serious? That isn't even the half of it."

"I mean, your mom and I have come to terms with the family in Houston. We don't ever plan on speaking to them again because of everything that happened, so don't feel guilty about that. Really. In fact, all those visits stressed me out anyway. I was never really a big fan of Houston."

But as my dad continued, my mother stood up from the table suddenly. She walked away from us with tears in her eyes.

"Look, your mother is still upset about her relationship with her brother, but it's been a year. She puts you first. We both do, so don't feel bad about your aunt and uncle. They can go to hell for all I care. Don't let them win. Don't let them take anything more from you."

With watery eyes, I desperately tried not to cry. I couldn't show my weakness to my dad and didn't want to get in another argument about food. I was too tired to do it again.

"Thanks," I said.

My mom walked back in with a tissue in hand and sat down at the table. She turned to me. "Neesha, I need you to know that you come first. No matter what. I am so sorry all of this happened, and it was completely unfair for you. My relationship with your uncle will never mean more to me than you do. I don't want you to think that it ever would. I trusted him to take care of you and he let me down. I can't forgive him for that, and they will never be in our lives again. It's for the best. I promise."

I looked down. "Thanks, Mom."

"So do you think we can try to make things better? We are fine without them. We need to be a family again. I know this must have been very hard on you, and I'm sorry if I made it any worse."

"I'll try. Thank you."

But it wasn't so easy to eat normally again. Pull it together, I told myself. You can eat again. But I couldn't.

I sloshed three spoonfuls of potatoes onto my plate, dripping with butter. I tried to hide my nerves. I sat next to my dad, horrified that this was a topic of conversation, hoping he wouldn't watch me eat.

I mashed up the salmon as small as I could and took tiny bites. I couldn't even taste food for pleasure anymore. I forced as much of the fish as I could down my throat, then I looked at the potatoes that I left for last. I twirled them on my fork as if they were pasta and gulped down a glass of water. I stood up and walked to the black fridge to refill my water glass, mentally preparing myself. As I sat back down, I could tell my parents were staring at me, hoping I would say something to make things better.

But I said nothing.

One forkful at a time, I placed the potatoes in my mouth and swallowed, trying not to taste them. Wanting to cry at that moment, I took a sip of water to pull myself together. How did I become so afraid of food? Why couldn't I simply swallow this bite and smile? They just said that everyone in Houston didn't matter anymore. Wasn't that enough to make it okay? Couldn't I eat normally again?

But the contradicting voice inside my head said, "Don't be a baby. Don't be weak. Don't give in to food."

I took another forkful of potatoes followed by a gulp of water, again and again, until my plate was clean. I was the last person to finish eating. I placed my plate by the sink and blurted out, "Thanks for dinner, it was really good." Not acknowledging the fact that the topic we avoided for months was out in the open.

I walked down the hall to my room as my thoughts rushed to every different place. How many calories did I just eat? I wasn't expecting to eat potatoes with butter! How long will it take to work that off? How much did all that food weigh? How much do I weigh?

Developing a migraine, I held my head in my hands as I shook my foot back and forth, trying to burn off a few calories before my sit-ups. I reclined on the bedroom floor and played my favorite playlist with Maroon 5 and Snow Patrol.

I could not stand that much food being in my body. I needed to punish myself for eating so much. I didn't care about Anita or Rob or my aunt and uncle, but I still cared about Will and Mark.

Because of that, I could not change my self-destructive habits—not for myself, not for my parents, not for my therapist, and not for my friends. Food now represented the two boys to me. Food was the two boys, and I still wasn't rid of them.

I had no other option.

Right then, I knew getting the food out of my stomach would give me a sense of relief, a moment of relaxation knowing it was gone. I glanced at the clock—8:30 pm. I tried to do sit-ups to distract myself from doing anything harmful, but I teetered between taking the laxatives or not. I needed to get the food out, fast. More than that, I wanted to feel some sort of freedom.

Embarrassed but grateful to be alone, I walked into my bathroom slower than usual. I opened the drawer and looked at the box of laxatives. Letting out a deep sigh, I felt control in my hands, and I decided I would go for it.

I popped them in my mouth. One. Two. Three. Four. Five.

I would have taken a sixth, but fear overtook me. I based my dosage purely off what I read online earlier in the hopes of getting all the food out. I hadn't taken them since the night of the big volleyball game that I didn't get to play in. I thought this time would not be as painful since I would be dispensing the salmon I just ate. Almost like I had thrown up the cake on my birthday right after.

As I waited for the pills to work, my self-hatred increased. I stumbled back to my room and cuddled with my two comforters in my bed. My empty emotions didn't allow me to think about anything. I simply had to wait.

I ignored the grumbling of my stomach, anticipating the vertical knife-slice down my stomach—the one I'd felt the last time I took these. The clock struck 9:00, then 9:30, and I continued to wait.

Suddenly, at 9:42 p.m., I felt a sharp blade cut through my stomach. The same urgency I had felt the previous time I took laxatives filled me, so I burst out of my bed and ran to the bathroom. Unable to breathe, I pulled down my pants and sat on the toilet, trembling, saliva drooling down my chin because of my clattering teeth. With my hands cupped to my face, I felt my cheekbones close to my fingertips.

As I let liquid out, it stung in the same way it did before. I shook twice as much as I had the last time, quivering like I was in the middle of a seizure. Suddenly, I slipped off the toilet and hit the floor. Coughing, I looked down at my bloated stomach. It was round and enormous. I couldn't believe it could look like that when I weighed so little. But my stomach would not let anything out despite the pain, despite the swelling.

I started screaming. I screamed the screams I should have screamed that New Year's Eve. The screams for help.

I wanted to give up. Hearing voices in my head, I recognized the calm sound of the heating lamp and tried to breathe. I lay on the floor until I felt a piercing pain through my stomach. Back to the toilet. Liquids burst out of me into the water, and I felt relief in my stomach. Still shaking but with more of a vigorous bounce, I tried to calm my boney legs down.

I burped for a few seconds, wondering how much air filled my stomach, and then vomit suddenly filled my throat. I turned my body around as fast as possible, fell to my knees on the bath mat, and bent over. Out spewed white and salmon-pink bile. Disgusted and gagging, choking on my own puke, I inadvertently made myself throw up more as I tried to spit it out.

After five minutes of puking, I fell back on the step next to the shower. I flushed the toilet and cleaned the vomit from the sides, throwing the toilet paper in before it flushed. But I didn't get to rest for long before my stomach cramped again. Back and forth three times

I went to the toilet, releasing all the liquids in my body. I reached up to flush the toilet again as I watched the colored water swirl down.

Finally, I thought it was over. I lay helplessly on the bath mat with my bloated stomach. I found enough energy to flush the toilet once again, determined to hide all the evidence of what happened, even if it was the last thing I did.

My poor body. I looked down at what I had become, humiliated. The back of my hipbones shot through my skin. I didn't look like myself. Faint noises came out of my mouth as I tried to scream as loud as I could for help, but I didn't care if my parents found me. I thought it was too late, anyway. I thought I was dying.

I tried to cry, but there were no tears coming.

I heard a growl from my stomach and moved back to the toilet one last time. I sat there with my entire torso balancing on my knees. My cheeks touched my kneecaps as they bounced up and down. I pushed as hard as I could to get whatever else was left in my body out of it. I couldn't smell much, considering my senses were dysfunctional in this state, but I could make out the stench of blood. I looked down in the toilet.

Blood gushed out of my body—not a thin stream like when I had taken laxatives before. It continued for about two seconds. Immediately afterward, I flushed the toilet again to hide any trace of that red liquid. Looking around the bathroom, I noticed only one drop of blood on the white tile and I wiped it up. I threw the toilet paper into the bowl and flushed down all the proof. No one would ever know what happened.

My body turned limp and collapsed back to the bath mat. I screamed even louder, "Help! Help! Mom! Dad!" But I couldn't even hear my own voice. I thought I was in a dream.

Keeping my eyes closed, I couldn't bear to see the blinding light above me.

Minutes later, I heard a knock on the door. "What's going on, Neesha?" my dad's voice demanded on the other side.

I tried to say something, anything, but all I could manage was, "Puhhlesss…"

My dad flung the door open. I couldn't even look up at him. I began to hyperventilate, coughing up little droplets of runny spit. My dad picked my fragile body up off the floor.

Then everything went dark.

28 ∘ *full circle*
december, 2006

I woke up in my bed the next morning, the bed I grew up in, and the bed I laid awake in every night for the past year. At fifteen, I knew I had lost my battle to erase this memory. My secret was out, and I was out of my mind. They wanted to take me to the hospital, but I had persuaded them to put me to bed.

A glass of water and my trash can were beside me. My mouth tasted like I ate a block of chalk, and my teeth felt like dried-out wood. I wore my pink tank top, the one from Texas, but it was no longer the original bright shade of pink it used to be. Now a dull peach color, it was looser than before. Looser than ever. I didn't want to be this person anymore. I didn't want to look like this anymore. All I wanted was my innocence, sanity, and youth back. As I began crying, I looked around my room. I closed my eyes and immediately thought about the exercise room and the boys' faces.

I looked down at my legs and saw that my body looked so different from a year ago. I felt weaker than I had in months, even weaker than New Year's Eve. I thought about how my body was shattered. I had lost my battle with myself. I thought I was winning. I did not anticipate this outcome.

I could not believe I had been so careless. My face, tight as plastic wrap over a container, did not feel like a face. It felt like a mask. Confused and devastated, I lost my identity. I lost myself. I had killed the person I used to be, the little girl who would laugh with her best friends, the little girl who looked up to her parents. I lost my way.

Being a typical fifteen-year-old again was all I desired. I wanted to be able to sleep in this bed and finally feel rested. No interrogations from detectives, no repeating the sexual terms I was forced to say on camera—none of it. I wished to have no worries in the world. I needed to be free from everything. I dreamed about kissing boys and being happy. I longed for the excitement that my friends felt while holding a boy's hand, with butterflies in their stomach. I wanted my first touch and first sexual experience to mean something to me.

I intended to forgive myself for what happened on New Year's Eve, but I only punished myself with guilt and destruction. Searching to come to terms with Houston, I turned to an obsession with food that drove me insane. Even as I numbly shifted underneath my comforter, I tried to convince myself that I was in control.

Lie.

I didn't have control; food controlled me. That night controlled my thoughts. But I now knew I would have to accept my past and move forward. It was part of me, but I needed to let it go.

I looked around my room once more while I fought my emotions and my stomach turned. How could being empty feel so comforting for so long, yet leave me emptier than ever?

I let out a sigh as tears continued to fall.

Starving myself was what I had wanted, but now I knew that working to achieve an impossible goal hurt far worse than failing. I had no sense of satisfaction as I lay in a bed that didn't feel like mine any longer. Nothing made me proud of myself anymore.

I couldn't even remember what it was like to be close with my mom and dad. I missed the year before, when we were a team. Now that was gone. It hurt to watch our relationship deteriorate, but I was determined to get it back.

I touched my dry, cracked lips as my heavy head fell to my chest.

Spotting my boney knees through my sheets, I knew this did not feel right anymore.

With no idea of how to move forward and change, I stared at my pink tank top—the top that once meant strength to me. The one that made me the girl I used to be before New Year's. Tears dropped onto the material.

How could I fix this?

I finally wanted help from my parents, my friends, and my therapist. I recognized my mistakes. I realized I couldn't live like this anymore. How could I have been so selfish? I should have confronted my problems instead of running away from them. I was ready to do that now.

But first, there was something I needed to do.

I reached over to my dresser and picked up a black ballpoint pen. A teardrop fell like the bitter sting of a bee as it wet my bed sheets. Grabbing the yellow notepad sitting next to the clock on my bed stand, I began to write.

29 ∘ *controlled*

Mark and Will,

You took away my childhood when I was fourteen.

I want you two to understand what it's like to be violated in the manner that you both violated me. What hurt me the most is that you blamed me for what happened when you knew I did nothing wrong.

Mark, I am ashamed to say I knew you, growing up. I wish I never did because I trusted you. Not only did you betray and assault me, but you also had the audacity to lie about it.

I convinced myself that this was my fault the second you put the blame on me. You were able to sleep peacefully while I lay wide-awake thinking about that memory. You were sleeping all those nights when I was getting rid of every liquid and piece of food from my body; when I was just trying to get rid of you. I was trying to get rid of your faces, your voices, and your minds.

You ruined the relationship with my parents when it was never their fault. You are the reason my aunt and uncle and I will never speak again. But I don't care anymore. You can have Houston and that part of my family.

You don't understand how truly malicious that night was. That exercise room will forever be in my mind, and I will never forget it as long as I live.

I have faced that night, and now I can finally put it behind me. My biggest regret is that I let you both get away with everything. I wish I did not hide, but I can't fix anything now—I can't take you to court. You got off so easily because I was too afraid.

I'm done being afraid. I spent months picking up the pieces of my life, trying to make sense of it all, but there is no way to make sense of it. I used to want the worst for you two, but you don't mean anything to me anymore. You never will again.

I have forgiven myself for that night and even for being so self-destructive. I refuse to live like this anymore. What you did to me controlled my life, every second of every day, for the past year. You were the reason behind every choice I made.

You controlled me.

But you won't control me anymore.

EPILOGUE ○ ten years later

I've been asked by many people, including my publisher and agent, how I was able to stop anorexia from consuming my life—how I fulfilled my promise to myself to no longer be controlled by what had happened with Mark and Will. These questions about my recovery made me oddly restless. I never intended to write a self-help book—just an honest account of the crime. When I was asked, "What changed you—what made the difference between a life of healing and a life of continual dysfunction?" I couldn't answer. In fact, when my publisher asked what happened in those years after the assault, I told her, "Nothing and everything."

Maybe it felt like nothing because the high stress was subsiding. I had been able to ask for help. I no longer had to put up a strong front for my family, but rebuilding the trust with my parents took years. The pain of trauma did not heal overnight, and I came to realize how greatly my parents had suffered. By the time I was sixteen, I had reconciled with my fourteen-year-old self, but the relationship with my parents wasn't so quick to improve. During my last two years of high school, there were still residual hard feelings between us. At that time, instead of hurting myself—and hurting them—I focused on my healing and recovery. I started to maintain a healthy weight and eventually joined the volleyball team again.

It was not until I left for college that we reached a point where we could openly discuss that year. A combination of time and distance allowed the three of us to move on from the past. The trials and tribulations of getting this book published also provided a helpful way for me to speak with my parents about the past and find some common ground. During the depths of my literary rejection, my dad told me, "Don't let perfection be the enemy of progress." I listened, and his advice changed my life. We are finally the team that we couldn't be when I was fourteen.

For me, it was never a matter of being skinny or fat—anorexia was the remnant of my sexual assault and a vehicle to satisfy my wish to simply disappear. When I no longer had a constant reminder of the crime, I felt more determined not to let the nightmare define me.

Looking back, I wish I'd never read those blogs or consumed myself in the self-destructive behavior of calorie counting and weight loss as a means of control. I never had control. I should have confided more in my friends and parents and let them help me.

Over the years I've become more open and found people who encouraged me to talk about my past in order to come to terms with it. Having the support of my friends during high school allowed me to live a life that had nothing to do with what happened that night. The people in my life have always been a great source of joy to me and are the reason I want to wake up in the morning. I have stayed close friends with Jane, Emma, and Brad.

Therapy changed my life in many ways. It wasn't until I started writing my book in college that I voluntarily went back to therapy. During that time, I was able to work through certain things in my past that I had never let go of before. Having a third party able to objectively help me work through the past allowed me to move forward. If it was not for therapy, I would not be able to say that I have made peace with my past.

The legal case was a pivoting point for me, not because of its nonexistent outcome, but because of how it affected my psyche. Once the case was moot, dismissed from my life, I was finally able to stop reliving that night every day on someone else's terms. I began to regain my strength.

When I went off to college in California at eighteen, I was able to start over. Life felt like a clean slate, but I also realized that I would need to deal with the aftershock of being attacked when I was so young. Then I began to write my story. After I graduated from college with a BFA in Creative Writing at twenty, I moved to New York City to pursue a writing career.

Now twenty-four years old, I spend my time living in the present. With the perspective of ten years, I now know that I have to put myself first. Not only that, but I need to have the courage to believe in myself. I am where I am today because of my determination to live my life, not to contort or suppress it.

After ten years, I have learned that perfection does not exist. I now know that I have to accept imperfection or I will never find love—love for myself, love for others, love for this world. It took me a long time to respect, love, and value myself in the way that I deserve. Looking back at my fourteen-year-old self, I see that running away and self-destruction only hurt me more.

Sexual assault is something that goes on every single day, and I want people to know that it is okay to talk about it. It is more than okay. It is helpful, it is right, and it is even necessary. I urge victims to stop blaming themselves. If you had an experience similar to mine, I am here to tell you that you are not alone, and what happened is not your fault. Not only that, you can have what you've always wanted. You can have love and peace of mind.

In the end, my redemption has been this book. It took me more than four years to begin to talk about my experience. I chose to push away my trauma and pretend nothing happened. But I woke up years later realizing that it was still hurting me and that I needed to fully express that hurt in order to let it go.

Until I began writing, I didn't realize that I could never fully move on with my life if I did not accept what happened and understand that I had been innocent. I hope victims can learn from my mistakes and ask for help instead of holding on to their fears. I have spent many hours in therapy working through the concept of blame only to realize it is not worth the energy. Instead, the process of getting this book published taught me how to love myself.

ACKNOWLEDGMENTS

Jeff, you took the first and only chance on that twenty-one-year-old writer when no one else would. You doubled down with me on this death bet and we have never looked back. Thank you for your unwavering confidence in me.

Naomi, you gave me the chance of a lifetime by deciding to publish this book. Thank you for believing in my message, my words, and most of all, me.

Katie Ford, you have spent your life fighting for women worldwide to get what they deserve. There is no bigger hero than that. It has been nothing but an honor to have your name on this book.

Brady, you know this book never would have happened if it were not for you. You have saved me more times than I can count, and you are without a doubt the love and light of my life.

Bronwyn, you are the most inspirational, loyal, brilliant person I have ever known. There has not been one day I couldn't count on you, and for that I owe you everything.

Erica, you have held my hand through this mentally unstable ride they call New York City. You are my other half and the greatest sister I never had.

Lizzy, we conquered detention, a jammed locker, school bullies, breakfast burritos, first loves, broken hearts, Los Angeles, Hurricane Sandy, and New York City. Growing up with you has been the greatest gift.

Royal, my boo, my bud, my joy. You made me believe in myself like no one ever has. You did it and you made me think I could, too. You amaze me, RY.

Reyn, Beth, Kit, you are three of the strongest women I have ever known. I will never know how I got you in my corner so early on, but for that I am grateful.

Jim Blaylock & Anna Leahy, you two have always been more than professors of writing to me. You have been my believers, my mentors, and my friends.

To my FB, forever ago, thank you.

I must give my undying love to my friends that made it all worth it: Maverick Adams, David Dye, Jay Caughren, Tatianna Duran, Ariel Ashe, Alex Borgeson, Louise Hearn, Sacha Jarmon, Ali Kuriyan, Carly Robinson, Kaitlyn Halamuda, Rachel Smith, Annie Clark, Martin Lynch, Claire Knebl, Elise Eberle, Sunny Tripathy, Courtney Groves, Alisha Brach, Joey Groff, Mollie Conlee, Faith Score, Georgia Bobley, Jennifer Wright, Peter Feld, Elspeth Walker, Mathew Lasky, Jessica Ritt, Dena Silver, Abby Haglage, Cara Zelas, Tim Mousseau, and Alyson Ahrns.

Mom, you have taught me to be brave, but more importantly, you have taught me to be kind. Thank you for your ineffable patience and your eternal love.

Dad, there is not a person in this world I admire as much as you. I could not ask for a better father or a better friend.

Nick, you have always been my guardian angel. I truly believe the world is a better place because you are in it.

To the Arter family, you have taught me how to laugh, especially in the face of great tragedy. There is no one I would rather spend this life with. Cheers to you, my wonderful family.

About the Author

Neesha Arter is a journalist and author in New York City. Her work has appeared in the *New York Times*, the *New York Observer*, *The Daily Beast*, *New York Magazine,* and other media.

She received her BFA in Creative Writing from Chapman University.

Controlled is her debut memoir.

CPSIA information can be obtained at www.ICGtesting.com
Printed in the USA
LVOW04s1518180815

450590LV00021BC/423/P